Team Sports for Fun and Fitness

This book is dedicated to all physical education teachers who have devoted their professional lives to enriching the health and wellness of all their students; not just the athletically gifted ones. Thank you!

By
Kathy Ermler
&
Joella Mehrhof

Mirror Publishing
PO Box 1708 • Emporia, KS

PO Box 1708
Emporia, KS   66801

ISBN 1-930359-06-3

Table of Contents

Principles of Teaching Team Sports at the Middle and Secondary Level

Principle #1: Throw out the rulebook. Students do not need to play on the regulation size playing field or court. Shorten the boundaries and create more playing areas. Keep the rules limited and simple. Use only the rules needed to play the activity. Do not give them the rules all at one time. Choose the most important rules and then add or modify the game.

Principle #2: Keep the numbers on the teams as small as possible. The smaller the number of students on a team, the more repetitions and the more practice each student is permitted during class. Try to decrease the number of students on teams to at least half of the recommended number of the original game.

Principle #3: Put out more equipment. Students do not need to use the exact piece of equipment to play a game. Due to budgetary constraints, few schools have an unlimited number of basketballs, volleyballs or rackets. However, by examining the objectives of the lesson, teachers can **SAFELY** substitute a different piece of equipment.

Principle #4: Let the students officiate and coach their own game. Team sports as lifetime activities are of a "pick-up" nature. Let the students learn how to call a game honestly and fairly as they are playing. By asking students to peer teach and coach, they become more self-directed and responsible for their own learning.

Principle #5: Make drills as game-like as possible. Practicing skills that do not relate to an aspect of the game do not transfer well. In order for positive transfer to occur and for students to see connections, the drills need to be closely related to game-like situations.

Principle #5: Teach to the outcomes. Remember, you are not trying to make basketball, volleyball, softball or football players out of the students. Instead these activities are used to reach the learning outcomes.

Outcomes

By the end of a team sport unit a student will be able to:

- Work together with others in a respectful and fair manner in a competitive situation.
- Maintain or improve health-related fitness
- Identify and apply motor skills utilized in common team sports.
- Develop an appreciation for new team sport activities.

Educational Opportunities

The teacher must design a team sport unit carefully in order to reach the stated outcomes. Just because the outcomes are related to a team sport unit, does not mean that by merely playing the game, a student will achieve these outcomes. Suggestions for educational opportunities that need to be included with team sports units include:

- Officiating opportunities
- Coaching opportunities
- Peer teaching of skills and strategies
- Introduction of new or unfamiliar team sports
- Progression of skill development, as well as the opportunity and time to develop skill
- Altered rules in order to reward and encourage the process not the product
- Encouragement and rewarding of sportsmanship and respect

Assessment

Outcomes and educational opportunities necessitate the need for an accurate and authentic assessment. Possibilities for assessment include:

- Rubric on sportsmanship
- The recording of heart rate, perceived exertion on a weekly basis
- Tournament results
- Student feedback on activities throughout the unit (written or oral)
- Fitness portfolio
- Development of offensive and defensive strategies
- Skill stations
- Peer and self skill assessment rubrics
- Responsibility check lists

Safety Guidelines and Alternative Equipment for Team Sport Areas

Safety guidelines for Basketball

1. Spacing of individuals
2. Force of passes
3. Loose basketballs on the floor

Alternative equipment to use in the Basketball unit

- Any ball that will bounce (volleyballs, playground, nerf balls, etc.)
- Hula-hoops taped to volleyball standards for baskets
- Adjustable goals

Safety guidelines for Lacrosse

1. Spacing of individuals
2. Use of soft balls in place of regulation lacrosse balls
3. Sticks usage, including no contact or limited checking
4. Safety areas between fields
5. Safe and appropriate shooting distance away from goalie

Alternative equipment to use in the Lacrosse unit

- Gallon milk jugs cut in half to make a scoop (tape edges with duck tape to prevent cuts)
- Stix ball sets
- Any small, soft ball (tennis ball, bean bag, puff ball) as the game ball
- Goalie creases spray painted on the grass
- Cones for goals
- Chip nets for goals

Safety guidelines for Hockey

1. Spacing of individuals
2. No sticks swung above shoulders
3. Use of soft balls or pucks in place of regulation hockey balls or hockey pucks
4. Safety areas between fields
5. Safe and appropriate shooting distance away from goalie

Alternative equipment to use in the Hockey unit

- Any small, soft ball (tennis ball, bean bag, puff ball) as the puck or ball
- Goalie creases or areas spray painted on the grass
- Brooms used instead of hockey sticks
- Pillo polos used instead of hockey sticks
- Nerf noodles used instead of hockey sticks
- Cones for goals
- Chip nets for goals

Safety guidelines for Volleyball

1. Spacing of individuals
2. Loose volleyballs on the floor
3. Safety areas between courts

Alternative equipment to use in the Volleyball unit

- Any ball light and safe enough to be passed with hands or forearms (beach balls, nerf balls, trainer balls, balloons, etc.)
- Bungee cord or rope for net
- Eye bolts screwed into the wall instead of standards

Safety guidelines for Softball

1. No throwing of the bat
2. Spacing of individuals
3. No sliding into bases
4. Use of a rag ball when no mitts are available
5. Safety areas between fields

Alternative equipment for use in the Softball unit

- Pillo polos for bats
- Flat bats
- Any soft, hittable ball (rag ball, all ball, tennis ball, nerf balls)
- Cones or poly spots for bases

Safety guidelines for Frisbee

1. Use of softer Frisbees when indoors
2. Spacing of individuals
3. Safety areas between fields

Alternative equipment for use in the Frisbee unit

- Soft or foam Frisbees
- Spinjammer Frisbees

Safety guidelines for Team Handball

1. Spacing of individuals
2. Use of junior team handballs or nerf balls
3. Safety areas between courts
4. Safe and appropriate shooting distance away from goalie

Alternative equipment to use in the Team Handball unit

- Any ball that is soft and bounces (junior team handballs, nerf balls)
- Tape or a mat for a goal

Safety guidelines for Football

1. Spacing of individuals
2. Safety areas between fields
3. Force of passes

Alternative equipment to use in the Football unit

- Footballs appropriate for the skill of the player - nerf footballs with lesser skilled players, junior footballs for smaller players, regulation footballs for advanced players
- Spray paint or cones to mark field lines

Safety guidelines for Soccer

1. Spacing of individuals
2. Safety areas between fields
3. Force of kicks
4. Possible use of nerf balls with lesser skilled players
5. Safe and appropriate shooting distance away from goalie
6. No tripping or kicking of opponent's shins

Alternative equipment to use in the Soccer unit

- Any balls that can be kicked safely (trainer soccer balls, nerf balls, playground balls)
- Cones for goals and field markers
- Spray paint marking off goalie area

Basketball

Basketball

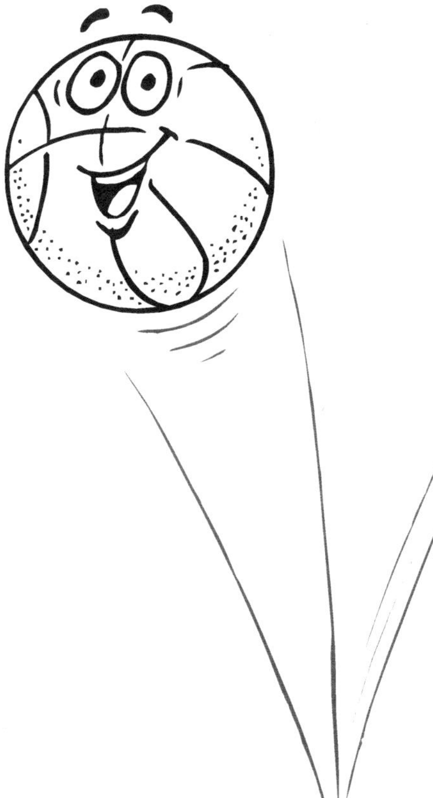

Basketball

Skill Progression

1. Dribbling
2. Defensive position
3. Passing - chest, bounce and overhand
4. Shooting - set shot, lay-up and jump shot
5. Rebounding
6. Offensive and defensive strategies

Ball Handing

Basic Ball Handling Activities

- Ball taps between hands
- Circle ball around the body
- Circle ball around the head
- Figure 8 around legs
- Wall passing
- Two-ball dribble
- Dribble the length of the court, shoot at the foul line
- Dribble the length of the court, lay-up on the left side
- Dribble from the right sideline, lay-up on the right side
- Free throws

The Big Fake Out

Equipment: CD Player and music Space Jam
Group Size: Individual
Description:

- Start the music
- Students pick up an imaginary basketball and perform basic basketball skills
- Examples
  1. Around the waist, head, legs
  2. Figure 8's
  3. Dribbling
  4. Passing
  5. Defensive slides
  6. Jump shots

Michael Jordan Challenges

Equipment: Ball for every pair, cones, check sheet
Group size: Pairs
Description:

- Have each pair attempt to see how many of the items they can complete in 10 minutes.

Challenges

1. Around the cone, to the foul line, dribble lay-up on the right side.
2. Around the cone, to the foul line, dribble lay-up on the left side.
3. Wall passing, 50 catches in a row.
4. Two-ball dribble 50 times in a row.
5. Two-ball dribble 50 times while on the knees.
6. Side shot after dribbling through three cones.
7. Weave in and out of the three cones, corner shot.
8. Lay-up right side then left side.
9. Five-dot shooting, all made 3,4,5,6,7 feet from the basket.
10. Hook shot from 3 feet.
11. Hook shot from 6 feet.
12. Dribble the length of the court, jump shot at the foul line.
13. Dribble the length of the court, jump shot right and left side of the foul line.
14. Dribble from the left sideline; lay-up on the left side.
15. Dribble from the right sideline; lay-up on the right side.
16. Dribble around the cone, foul shot.
17. Dribble around the cone, 3-point shot.
18. Run around the gym 2-ball dribbling.
19. Run around the gym 2-ball dribbling backwards.

Skill Drills

Poker Chip Pass

Equipment: 1 Ball per pair and a poker chip or penny
Group size: Pairs
Description:

- Have partners stand facing each other about 10 feet apart.
- They should put the poker chip in-between them (about 5 feet away from either partner).
- On a signal, the pairs begin to bounce pass attempting to hit the poker chip and move it closer to the other person.
- After about a minute stop and see to which person the poker chip is closer.
- Rotate one line and compete against a new partner.

Giant Jacks

Equipment: Two hula-hoops for each team, one ball that bounces and 10 beanbags for each team.

Group Size: 3 or 4

Description:

- Teams should line up behind a starting line.
- A hoop is placed behind each team and another hoop is about 30 feet away.
- The 10 beanbags are placed in the away hoop.
- Teacher calls which of the following jack games will be played.

Baby Jacks

1. On a signal, the first person on each team dribbles the ball toward the hoop.
2. The student will toss the ball, pick up a beanbag and attempts to catch the ball after one bounce. If successful, s/he dribbles back and places the beanbag in the hoop behind the team and gives the ball to the next player.
3. The next player does the same thing.
4. If unsuccessful, the student leaves the beanbag and dribbles back to the next person.
5. The object is to get all of the beanbags back to their line.

Crack the Egg

1. On a signal, the first person on each team dribbles the ball toward the hoop.
2. The student tosses the ball, picks up a beanbag, "cracks" or taps it on the ground and attempt to catch ball after one bounce. If successful, the student dribbles back and places the beanbag in hoop and gives the ball to the next player.
3. The next player does the same thing.
4. If unsuccessful, the student leaves the beanbag and dribbles back to the next person.

Pigs Over The Fence

1. On a signal, the first person on each team dribbles the ball toward the hoop.
2. The student tosses the ball, picks up a beanbag and throws it over his/her arm to the outside of the hoop. S/he then catches the ball after one bounce. If successful, s/he dribbles back and places the beanbag in the hoop and gives the ball to the next player.
3. The next player does the same thing.
4. If unsuccessful, the student leaves the beanbag and dribbles back to the next person.

2 Passes
Equipment: Balls for 1 team, 4 different color pinnies
Group Size: 4 teams
Description:

- The object of this activity is to complete two passes with people from the other two teams.
- Divide the class into 4 teams. Each team has a different color pinnie.
- For round one, the red team plays defense and the green, blue and yellow team attempt to complete two passes with the people on the other teams. (For example, a green player must complete a pass with a blue player and then a yellow player).
- Every player on one of the offensive teams should be given a basketball.
- If a person completes the two passes, then s/he gets one point.
- Go for one minute and change defensive teams.

Attack of the Scooters
Equipment: 1 Scooter and 1 basketball per pair
Group size: Pairs
Description:
- The partners with the basketball start on one side of the basketball court.
- The partners with the scooters are scattered around the court.
- The object is to try and dribble the ball back and forth across the court without being tagged by the players on the scooters.
- If a dribbler is tagged, s/he must dribble the basketball one time around the basketball court before re-entering the game.
- Switch roles every minute.

Balloon Pop

Equipment: 1 Ball per group and 3 balloons per group
Group size: 3
Description:

- Teams of 3 should find a basket at which to shoot.
- One person stands behind the baseline with a balloon.
- The other two players are trying to sink free throws. Every time one of the players sinks a free throw, the person with the balloon gives the balloon one puff of air.
- This can be a competitive activity (first team to break the balloon wins) or time the entire class to see how quickly all balloons can be broken.
- Switch and put a new person behind the end line.

Addition 21
Equipment: 1 Basketball for every group
Group size: 4
Description:

- The object of the game is to be the first group to score 21 points.
- Divide the students into groups of 4. Each team is assigned to a basket.
- The first person on each team shoots a free throw (two points if the shot is made).
- If the shot is not made, the next person in the line shoots.
- If the shot is made, the person can shoot a lay-up (one point if the shot is made).
- Whether the lay-up is made or missed, the next person in line shoots.
- The team must get 21 points exactly without going over. If they do, they go back to 0.

Partner Pass Tag
Equipment: Ball per pair, music with intervals of silence
Group Size: Pairs
Description:

- Have each pair get a ball and find a spot anywhere in the gym.
- When the music begins, the pair begins to pass the ball back and forth with each other.
- When music stops, whoever has the ball, chases the person without the ball (walking only).
- If the person is tagged, the chaser puts the ball down and the new chaser picks it up and does 10 cross over dribbles and then chases the other person.
- When the music comes back on, they begin passing again.

60 Second Superbounder
Equipment: 1 Ball per pair
Group size: Pairs
Description:

- One player starts at the free throw line. The partner starts under the basket with the ball.
- On a signal, the rebounder throws the ball to the shooter.
- The shooter takes a shot and then moves anywhere on the court.
- The rebounder catches ball and throws it to the shooter.
- Continue this sequence for one minute.
- After one minute, the rebounder becomes the shooter and the shooter becomes the rebounder.
- Combine the total of the pair and have them try to beat their score each round.

Dribble Tag
Equipment: 1 Ball per person
Group Size: Individual
Description:

- The object is for the students to attempt to knock away some else's basketball while maintaining control of his/her own basketball.
- If person has his/her ball knocked away, s/he should go to the sideline and perform some type of ball handling skill to get back in the game.
- Play a second round and reduce the size of the court.

3 to Score
Equipment: 1 Ball per group
Group size: 3
Description:

- Two teams of 3 should position themselves at a basketball goal.
- Designate a shooting line. Each team has its own basketball.
- On the signal, each team begins shooting and following up its own shots for rebounds.
- The first team to make three baskets scores one point.
- Play to 5 points or for 2 minutes and then rotate teams.

Basketball Golf

Equipment: Basketballs, cones or poly spots
Group Size: Pairs
Description:

- Before class, establish a nine-hole golf course in the gym.
- Use cones or poly spots as the tee off spots.
- Have students find a partner and assign each pair to a tee off hole.
- One of the students tees off by shooting the ball from the tee off spot.
- If the shot is missed, that student must rebound it quickly and shoot from the point at which s/he catches the ball.
- Once the basket is made, the other person tees off.
- The object of the activity is to have the lowest score at the end of the nine holes.
- A sample score sheet is listed below.

Golf Score Card		
Hole	**Name**	**Name**
#1		
#2		
#3		
#4		
#5		
#6		
#7		
#8		
#9		
Total		

Scoring

- **Hole in One** = Basket made in 1 shot -4 under Par = **1 point**
- **Double Eagle** = Basket made in 2 shots - 3 under Par = **2 points**
- **Eagle** = Basket made in 3 shots - 2 under par = **3 points**
- **Birdie** = Basket made in 4 shots - 1 under Par = **4 points**
- **Par** = Basket made in 5 shots = **5 points**
- **Bogey** = No basket made - 1 over Par **= 6 Points**

Pass and Go
Equipment: 1 Ball per group, poly spots
Group size: 3
Description:

- Put poly spots down in the center of playing area (1 for every group).
- Put the ball on top of the poly spot.
- One of the group members starts at the centerline. One member starts at the foul line. One member starts on the end line.
- On a signal, the centerline person picks up the ball, passes to the player at the foul line, and follows the pass.
- The foul line person passes the ball back to the centerline player who can dribble in and shoot.
- The shooter must get his/her own rebound.
- Meanwhile, the person behind the base line runs to the centerline to receive a pass from the shooter.
- The shooter runs to the foul line. The foul line player runs to become the baseline person.

Basketball Shootout
Equipment: 1 Ball per group
Group size: 3
Description:

- This activity is a simple shooting drill.
- All group members must make a lay-up before moving to spot #2.
- Spot #2 is free throw. All team members must make this shot before moving to #3.
- Spot #3 is the 3 point line. All team members must make this shot before moving to #4.
- Spot #4 is half court. All team members must make this shot before the task is completed.

Around the World
Equipment: 1 Ball per game
Group Size: Pairs
Description:

- One of the partners starts with a lay-up on one side. If s/he makes the shot, then s/he goes on to the next spot. If s/he misses, then that person can take a chance shot anywhere on the court.
- If the chance shot goes in, the player continues on to the next marked spot.
- If the chance is missed, the player turns the ball over to the partner.
- The first person to complete all spots is the winner.

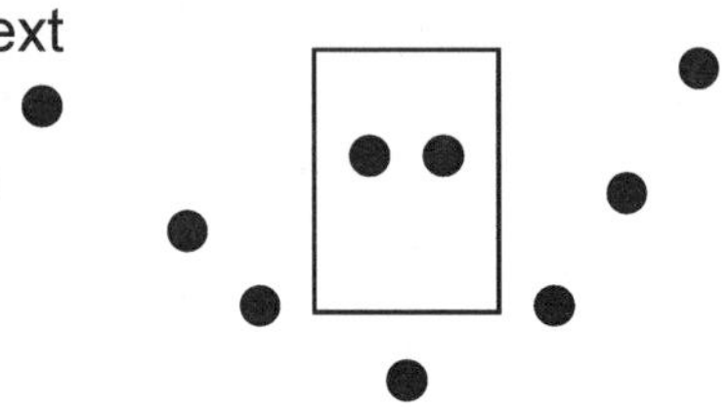

Keep Away
Equipment: 1 Ball per game, pinnies
Group Size: 4
Description:

- The object of the game is to make as many consecutive passes as possible without losing control to the opposite team.
- Each defensive player must stay with a designated opponent.
- If the ball is intercepted, give it back to the offensive team and have them begin counting again.
- Go for one minute and then give the possession to the opposite team.

Mass Pass

Students should get a partner and arrange themselves like the diagram below. A variety of ball handling skills can be developed. The person on the inside of the square has a ball. On a signal, the inside person passes to partner and then the partner passes the ball back to partner. The person on the outside of the square must move across the circle to find a new person to receive a pass from. The outside person continues to move to new passers for 30 seconds. Change the inside and the outside people and repeat the process. Examples follow:

Chest Pass
Bounce Pass
Overhand Pass
Dribbling

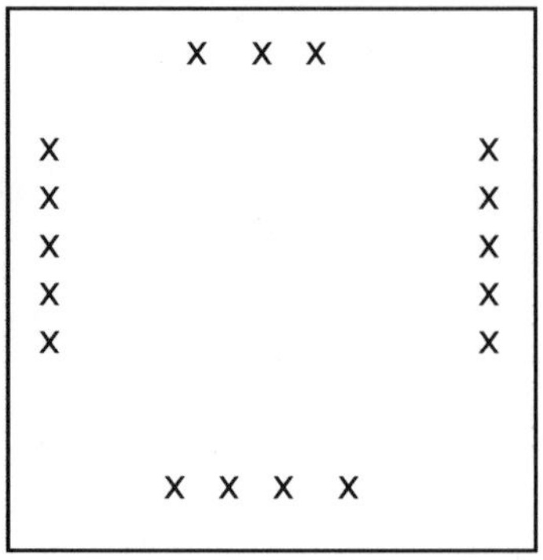

Obstacle Dribbling
Equipment: Signs for obstacle course and basketballs
Group Size: Two equal groups
Description:

- Each student should have a basketball or a ball that bounces.
- The object is to be the first team to have all of its team members complete the obstacle course.
- Twin obstacle courses should be created - one on each half of the gym. Each student should be assigned to a station to begin the course.
- On a signal all students complete the station to which they were assigned and then they move to the next one.
- The students must dribble the basketball throughout the entire course.

Sample course:

- Run to half court and back
- Ten figure-eights through the legs
- Slide from sideline to sideline
- Run around the circle at the free-throw lane
- Run to the end line
- Eight sit-ups
- Run diagonally across the gym
- Ten jumping jacks
- Pass ball around waist ten times
- Run a lap
- Five chest passes against the wall
- Run backward to half court
- Run across the low beam
- Kneel and dribble around the body five times
- Run a lap

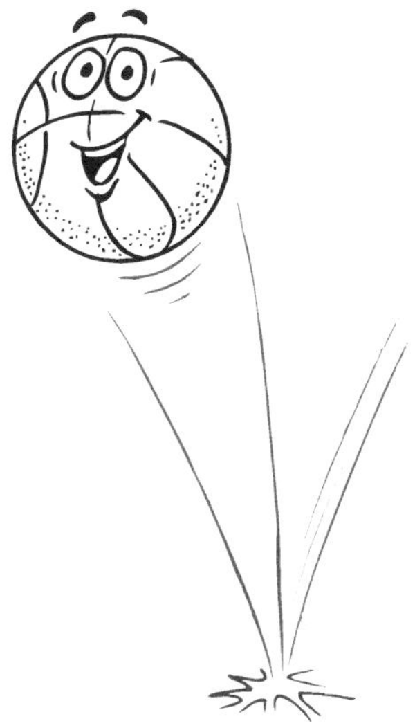

Steal the Balls
Equipment: 20 Balls, 2 hula hoops
Group Size: Two equal groups
Description:

- One hoop is placed at each end of the gym. Inside each hoop are 10 balls.
- The centerline is the dividing line for the two teams.
- 2 to 4 players on each team wear pinnies.
- The object of the game is to run across the centerline and get one ball at a time and bring it back to your team's hoop.
- When students cross the centerline, any player on the opposite team who is wearing a pinnie can tag that student.
- When tagged, the student puts the ball back in the opponent's hoop and returns to his/her half.
- The ITS are not allowed to guard the hoop area.
- Play 2-minute games.

Bowling Pin Call the Shot

Equipment: Bowling pin, 1 ball per group

Group Size: 4

Description:

- Place a bowling pin in the center of the gym.
- Students should be divided into groups of four.
- The object of the game is to score points by knocking over a bowling pin and shooting different types of shots at a basket.
- The rules are:
    1. The first person in each line rolls a basketball at the bowling pin. If the pin is missed, the player runs and retrieves the ball and gives it to the next person in the line. The next person in that line tries to knock the pin over.
    2. This process continues until someone on one of the teams knocks the pin over. This team scores one point.
    3. After the pin is knocked over, every team member runs to an assigned basket and shoots for one minute using a designated type of shot (lay-up, free throw, 3 point, jump shot).
    4. Each team keeps a total of the number of shots they make (one point for each made shot).

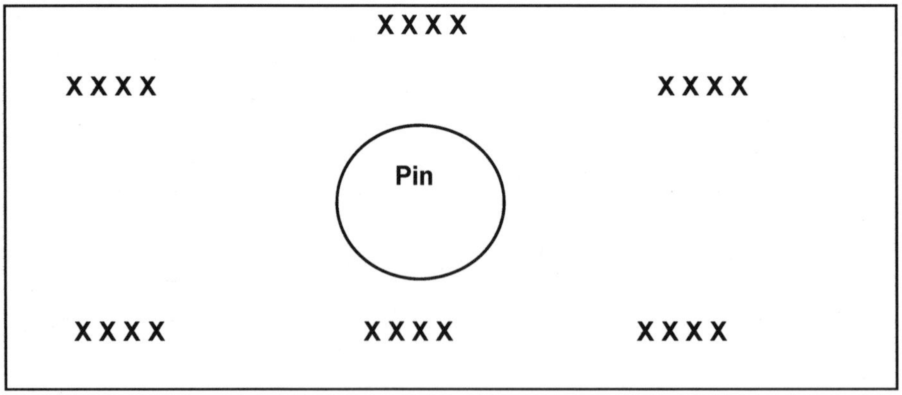

Quick Spots

Equipment: 5 Poly spots per game, 1 ball per game, pinnies

Group size: 4

Description:

- The object of the game is to score a point by passing a ball from a poly spot and catching a ball on another spot. Three successful throws and catches = 1 point.
- One team has the ball and may move anywhere in the designated area.
- The offense attempts to pass the ball from a spot to someone else standing on another spot.
- The defense tries to block or intercept the pass.
- If the defense gains possession of the ball, they immediately become the offense.

Hotshots

Equipment: Basketball per pair, tape or poly spots to mark shooting spots

Group size: Pairs

Description:

- The pairs should mark different spots around the basket using the tape or polyspots.
- One player is the shooter, and the other is the counter.
- A shooter gets points for each basket s/he makes. A lay-up is worth 1 point, baseline or free throws are worth 2 points, and shots from the side of the key are 3 points.
- A player may shoot only two lay-ups at a time, and then s/he must go to another spot. Once s/he takes another shot, s/he can go back and shoot two more lay-ups.
- The shooter must get his/her own rebound.
- Play a 1-minute round and then have the partner try to beat the score.

Basket O'Rama

Equipment: 1 Ball per pair

Group Size: Pairs

Description:

- Two pairs at each basket will challenge each other.
- One member from each pair shoots as rapidly as possible using any type of shot.
- The player who makes five baskets is the winner and their team gets 1 point.
- The other two players now do the same thing.
- Play 5 points or 3 minute games and rotate the teams.

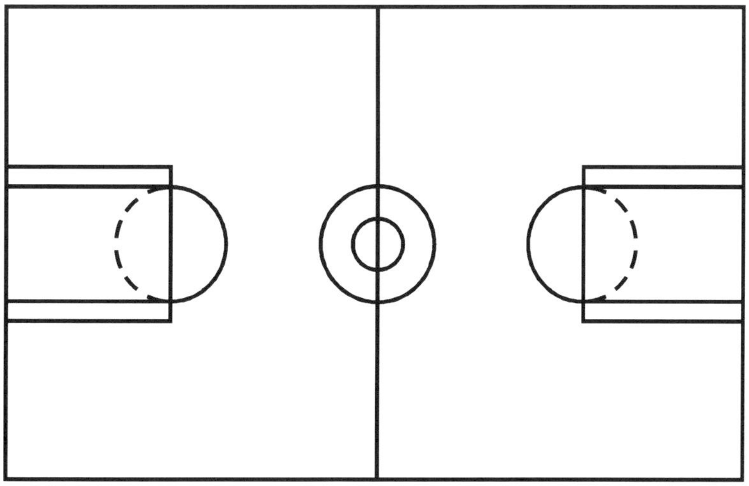

Lead-up Games

Clothes Pin Basketball
Equipment: 1 Basketball for each game, pinnies, clothespins,
Group Size: 4
Description:

- Divide the class into teams of 4. Assign 2 teams to a given playing area.
- On a signal, the teams to pass the ball to their other team members while calling out the number of passes.
- Teams score points by successfully passing the basketball five consecutive times.
- The person who catches the fifth pass, yells SCORE and hands the ball to the opposing team.
- When this happens, the team gets to collect a clothespin and clips it on his/her shirt.
- Play 5-minute rounds and rotate teams to a different area.
- Count the number of clothespins for each team at the end of a designated time.
- Return clothespins to the teacher and play another round.

Spasketball
Equipment: 1 Nerf ball per game, pinnies, hula-hoop
Group size: 4
Description:

- This game is a combination of speedball and basketball.
- Play half court games with one team starting at half court to begin the game.
- Hang the hula-hoop from the basket.
- No one may dribble the ball.
- Once the ball touches the floor, the ball must be played like a soccer ball until it is kicked or lifted back into the air.
- Scoring: 2 points for a basket, 1 point for touching the rim, 1 point for throwing it through the hula hoop.

Alarm Clock
Equipment: Basketball per group, tape with music and silence
Group Size: Teams of 4
Description:

- Each group of 4 forms a circle somewhere in the gym.
- When the music starts, the group begins passing the ball randomly around the circle, making sure that everyone is receiving the ball.
- When the music stops, each group lines up quickly behind the person with the ball.
- The ball is passed overhead from player to player.
- After it gets to the last person, the entire group runs to a basket and shoots (lay-ups, free throws, set shots) until music comes on.
- See how many shots can be made before the music comes back on.

Aerobic Basketball
Equipment: 1 Ball per game, pinnies
Group size: 3
Description:

- There are three teams per basket.
- One team plays offense, one plays defense and one team waits behind the end line.
- The object of the game is for the offense to score as many times as they can before the 30 seconds expires.
- If the offense scores, the ball is given right back to the offense at top of the key.
- At the end of 30 seconds, the offense goes off, defense becomes the offense, and waiting team plays defense.
- Play 5-minute games and then rotate the teams to different baskets.

Backboard Bombers
Equipment: Nerf balls for each game, pinnes
Group Size: 4
Description:

- The object is to pass the ball to teammates and score points by throwing the ball and hitting the backboard or making a basket.
- If the ball goes through the hoop = 3 points
- If the ball hits the backboard = 1 point
- However, points scored on a given shot are NOT COUNTED if the defensive team is able to catch (rebound) the ball before it touches the floor.
- Other rules
  1. No dribbling the ball
  2. Ball can only be held for 3 seconds
  3. No contact

Champs and Challengers
Equipment: 1 Ball per game
Group size: 3
Description:

- One group is the offensive team. One is the defensive team. The third team is waiting behind the base line.
- If the offensive team makes the shot, they stay on the court and the defensive team leaves.
- If the offensive team misses and loses possession of the ball, then the defensive team becomes the offense and the waiting team enters as the defensive team.
- Continue sequence for 5 minutes and rotate the teams.

6 Goal Basketball
Equipment: 1 Basketball per group, pinnies, flags
Group size: 4
Description:

- The object of this game is to score at all the baskets other than the one the team is defending.
- The teams should leave one player back on defense and the other three travel to the other baskets to score.
- Once the team scores, they take the color flag of the team they scored against.
- As soon as one team has all 5 flags, the game is stopped and flags replaced.
- Have a new person stay as the defender each time.

Generic Basketball
Equipment: 1 Playground ball per game, pinnies
Group size: 4
Description:

- Similar to regular basketball except:
    1. Players are only allowed to have the ball for 3 seconds (no matter if they are dribbling or not)
    2. The ball must be bounced off the floor into the basket
- Scoring
    1. Ball hits backboard = 1 point
    2. Ball hits rim = 2 points
    3. Ball goes through hoop = 3 points

Basketball Pyramid

Equipment: Pyramid board, name tags, basketballs (2 per basket), mark 5 spots at each basket

Group size: Pairs

Description:

- Pairs challenge another pair of partners to a game.
- The first partner from each pair shoots from each of the 5 spots, starting on opposite sides. S/he must shoot from spot #1 until the basket is made or the person has shot 10 times.
- S/he then does the same thing from spot #2,3,4, and 5. The other partner rebounds for the shooter.
- Once the shooter has completed his/her turn at spots #1-5, then the other partner shoots from 5, 4, 3, 2, and 1.
- At the same time this is taking place, the other pair is shooting from spots 5, 4,3, 2, 1,and then spots 1, 2, 3, 4, 5.
- The first team to complete all 10 spots is the winner and advances up the pyramid board.

Rules of Pyramid

1. The teams try to work their way to the top of the tournament chart and then maintain that position.
2. At the start of the tourney, no team occupies a position on the chart. Each team is free to challenge any other team to a match.
3. Winners are then placed on the lowest rung of the chart.
4. A team advances to a higher level by winning a match from another team at the same level.
5. The team reaching the top of the chart must defend its position by meeting challenges from the two teams directly below unless it has already competed against these teams.
6. If the top team is defeated, it exchanges positions with the victor.
7. Variation: Teams may challenge 1 row above when no free spaces remain on that row. If victorious, the challenge team changes places with its opponent.

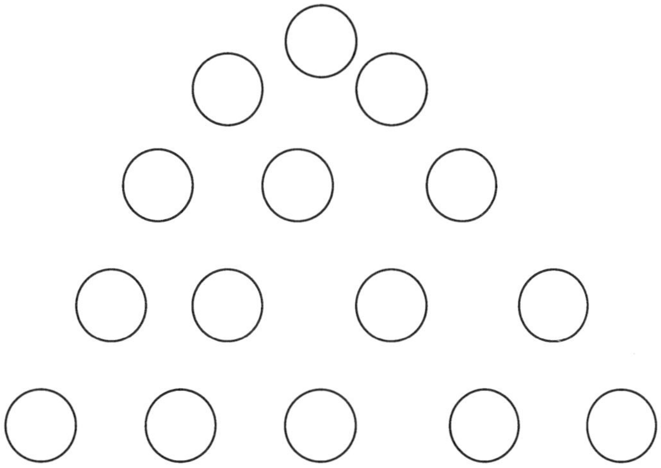

Top of the Hill
Equipment: 1 Ball per group, pinnies
Group size: Pairs
Description:

- Rank each basket playing area. Rank one court as Top of the Hill.
- To begin the game, players draw lots to see on which court they start.
- Play 3-minute games. The winning team moves to the next highest court, and the losing team stays on the court.
- At the Top of the Hill, winners stay and losers go down to the last ranked court.

5 on 5 All Star
Equipment: 1 Ball per game, pinnies
Group size: 3
Description:

- Regular basketball rules apply.
- The opponents get to name the player from the opposing teams who gets 3 points for every made shot. This person is called the All Star.
- Play 5 minute games and change opponents.

Football

Football

Skill Progression
1. Passing and catching
2. Handoffs
3. Centering and snapping
4. Defensive positioning
5. Offensive and defensive strategies

Basic Ball Handling Activities
- Passing and catching with partner
- Center snaps with handoffs with partner
- Underhand spins with partner

Cross-Country Football
Equipment: 1 Ball per pair
Group Size: Pairs
Description:
- Give each pair a ball.
- Describe or explain the running course.
- Give the students a skill (hiking, handoffs, passing, etc). They should work on the skill as they run the course. Have students pass the ball back and forth over the course.

Skill Drills

Flag Football Tag
Equipment: Colored flag belts (2 different colors)
Group Size: Two equal groups
Description:
- Divide the class into two groups and give different colored flag football belts to each team.
- The object of the game is for the players to successfully carry their football from one goal line to the other goal line without having their flags pulled.
- To start the game, one team (offense) lines up on the goal line. Each person on this team should have a football.
- The defense stands anywhere they want in the middle of the field.
- On a signal, the offensive team starts to run toward the other goal line.
- If a person with a football gets his/her flag pulled, that person puts the ball on the ground and walks or jogs to the goal line.
- Persons who successfully carry the football across the goal line without their flags being pulled score one point for their team.
- Switch offense and defense at the end of each run.

Partner Catch
Equipment: Football for every pair
Group Size: Pairs
Description:

- Have partners face each other and stand about 10' apart.
- On a signal, begin passing the ball back and forth with each other for 30 seconds.
- After 30 seconds, have one line rotate down one person to the right.
- Continue until each person is back to his or her original partner.

Crash and Burn
Equipment: Football for every pair, flag for each student
Group size: Pairs
Description:

- Have students arrange themselves in four lines. Line 1 should face line 2 and line 3 should face line 4. Each line is about 10' apart.
- Students begin to pass the football back and forth with partner.
- On signal "Crash" or whistle, the student with the ball should run away from the partner without the ball for about 10 seconds. The partner without the ball attempts to pull the flag of the partner with the ball. (Music intervals can be used instead of whistle or calling out crash).
- If the partner with the ball gets his/her flag pulled, then the other person gets 1 point.
- If the person with the ball does not get his/her flag pulled, then s/he gets one point.
- At the end of 10 seconds, come back to the line and begin passing again.
- Have the students rotate down one person to the right for the next round.

3's Down The Field
Equipment: 1 Football per group
Group size: 3
Description:

- This activity works on hiking and hand-offs.
- Arrange the 3's along the sideline of the football field.
- They should be arranged in back, center and quarterback positions.
- On a signal, the center hikes the ball to the quarterback, who hands off to the back, who runs 5 yards in front of center and becomes the new center.
- Center goes to quarterback, quarterback to back, and back to center.
- Go from sideline to sideline.

Mirrors

Equipment: Ball for each pair
Group size: Pairs
Description:

- The first student runs a set distance, turns to the partner, receives a pass, and then runs back to the start.
- As soon as the partner gets back to the start, the other one hikes the ball and then runs the same distance.
- Do the shuttle pattern a set distance or for a set amount of time.

Mass Pass

Students should get a partner and arrange themselves like the diagram below. A variety of ball handling skills can be developed. The person on the inside of the square has a ball. On a signal, the inside person passes to the partner and then the partner passes the ball back to partner. The person on the outside of the square must move across the circle to find a new person to receive a pass from. The outside people continue to run for 30 seconds. Switch the inside and outside people and repeat the process.

Centering
Passing
Blocking

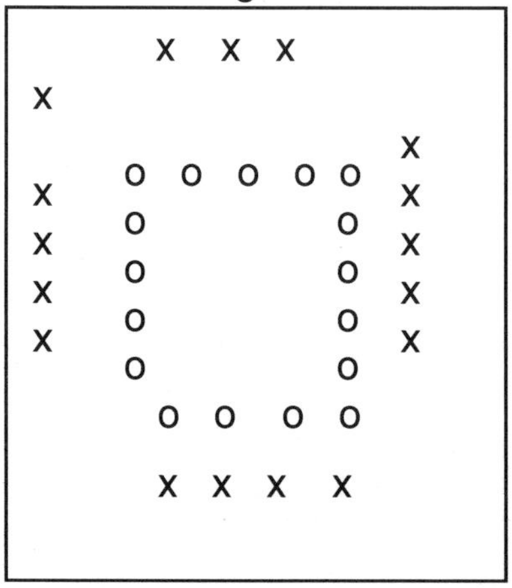

3's Tag

Equipment: Football for every group
Group size: 3
Description:

- Two players stand 10 feet away from a goal line (marked by cones) and begin to toss football back and forth.
- The third person stands near the goal line and calls a number between 1 and 10.
- The two players tossing begin to count every time they throw.
- They throw and catch until they reach the number called by the third player.
- The player making the final catch must run with the ball and carry it across the goal line.
- The number caller attempts to tag the player before s/he can run over the goal line.
- If the runner makes it, then s/he gets a point. If the tagger gets the runner, s/he gets a point.
- Rotate positions and play games of 5 points.

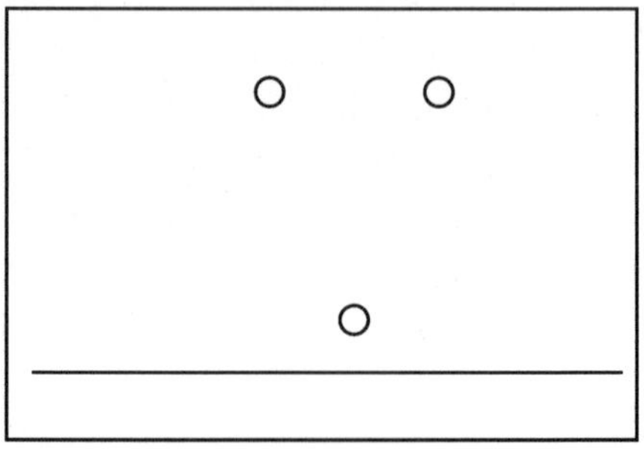

Pass Pattern With and Without Defenders
Equipment: Pass pattern sheets, 1 ball per group
Group size: 4
Description:

- Give each group a pass pattern sheet and have them practice the patterns indicated below.
- Indicate that they will use these patterns in the next game.

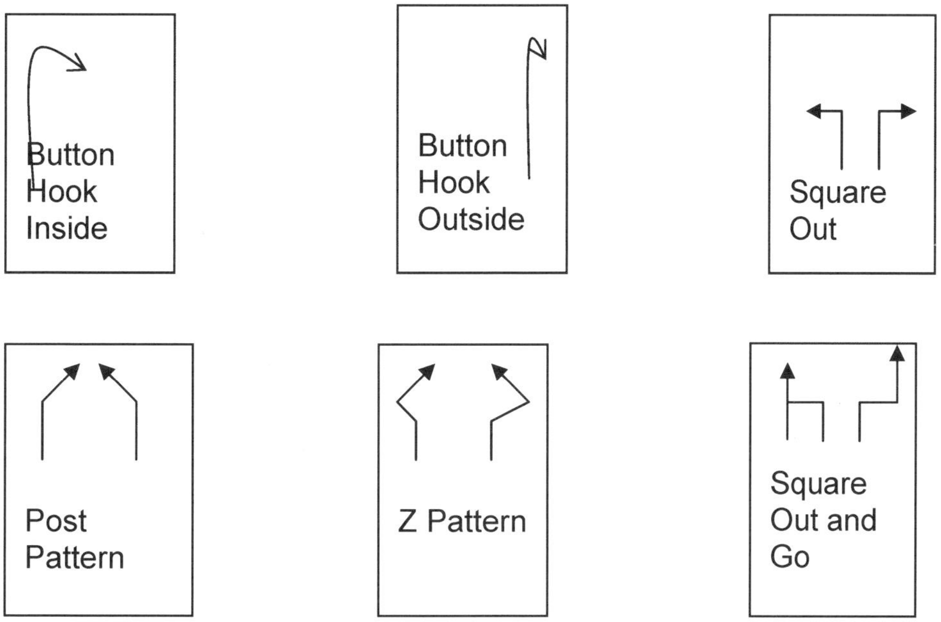

Center, Pass, Receive, Defend
Equipment: 1 Ball per group
Group size: 4
Description:

- Have group members assume the following roles - center, quarterback, receiver, defender.
- The center snaps the ball to the quarterback.
- As soon as the quarterback has the ball, the receiver runs forward and tries to catch a pass.
- The defender moves at the same time and tries to intercept the pass.
- Rotate positions and continue until all players have played every position.

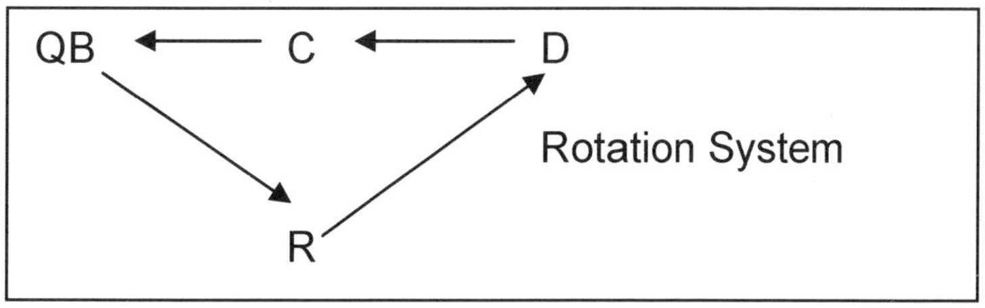

Single Football

Equipment: 1 Ball and 2 cones per group
Group Size: 4
Description:

- Give each group a ball.
- One player is chosen to be the runner.
- The runner stands at one of the cones with the ball.
- The other 3 people spread out in the field area.
- When the runner is ready, s/he throws ball in the designated area.
- The runner must run from the starting cone to the other cone and back without being caught.
- The fielders can only catch the runner by tagging the runner with the ball.
- Rotate new runners each throw.

Target Ball

Equipment: Footballs, empty tennis cans or pins or cones
Group Size: Pairs
Description:

- Pairs should set up the field as shown below.
- The object is to knock more pins over than the other set of pairs they are challenging.
- On a signal, one person hikes the ball to the other partner who then must run a lap with the football around the outside of the playing area.
- When that person returns, s/he passes the ball at the pins and attempts to knock one over.
- Whether made or missed, the person retrieves the ball and then hikes the ball to the waiting partner.
- The partner repeats the process.
- Continue for a set amount of time or until all pins are hit.
- Have pairs challenge a new pair.

= Pins

= Hiking Stations

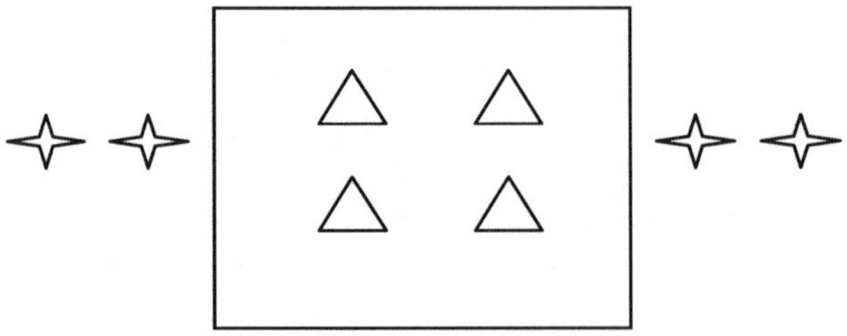

Boundary Football
Equipment: Footballs and cones
Group Size: Two equal teams
Description:

- Before the game begins, mark out a playing area.
- The offensive team lines up on the sideline. The defensive team spreads out anywhere in the fielding area.
- To begin the game, a person on the offensive team throws the ball anywhere into the field.
- After the throw, the entire team must run across the field to the other boundary line.
- The defensive team must field the ball and then attempt to tag as many players as possible by touching them with the ball.
- Defenders may run to tag runners or throw the ball to other fielders to tag the runners. Runners who are tagged freeze until runners have either made it to the other boundary line or have been tagged.
- Each tagged player counts as one point for the defensive team.
- Switch offense and defense after every run. The use of more than one football can also be incorporated.

Pass and Catch
Equipment: 1 Football per group
Group size: 5
Description:

- Have one team on one half of a small grid field and another team on the other side of the field.
- The game involves passing and receiving.
- One team is in possession of the ball. That team passes the ball over the centerline into the opponent's area.
- The opponent who is closest to the ball tries to catch it.
- Whoever catches the ball passes right back.
- If the ball is dropped, then the team that passed the ball receives a point.
- Play for 3 minutes and rotate teams.

Lead-up Games

4 on 2 Keep Away
Equipment: 1 Football per group
Group Size: 6
Description:

- Use small grid fields.
- Four people play offense and two people play defense.
- The object of this activity is for the four people playing offense to keep the ball for 10 passes. If they get 10 passes, that offensive group gets 1 point.
- Switch offensive and defensive people every two minutes.

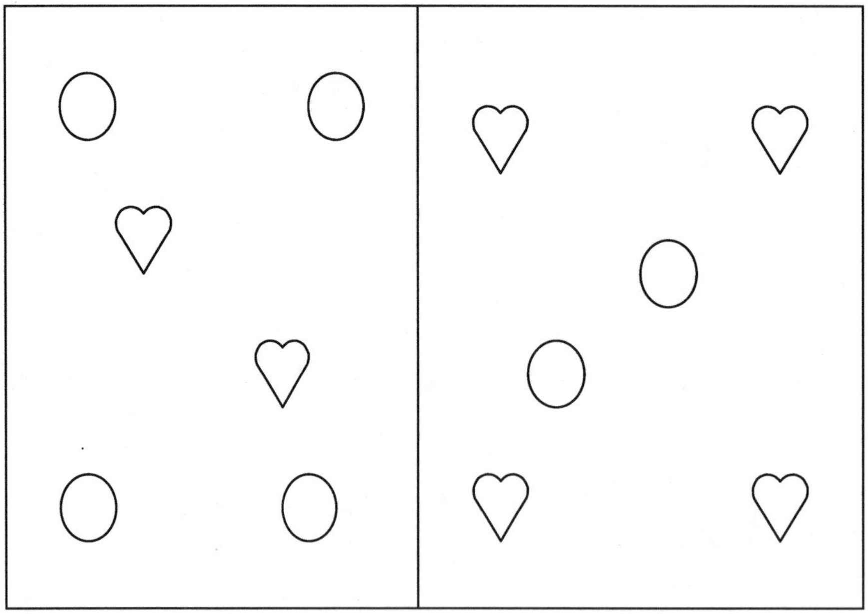

Aerobic Football

Equipment: 1 Football per group, flags for different teams

Group size: 5

Description:

- Use small grid fields.
- Have two teams play on each field.
- The game begins with a center snap in the middle of the field from one of the teams.
- The offense is allowed to pass, hand-off or run with the ball (eliminate the run if game does not go well).
- A player is only allowed possession of the ball for 3 seconds.
- To score, the ball must be passed and caught behind the goal line. The ball cannot be run over the end line.
- The defense stops the offense by tagging or deflagging the person with the ball.
- The person who was tagged immediately centers the ball and play continues. Teams do not need to be on side.
- Defense may steal the ball when it is in the air, but cannot knock or strip it from another player.
- If ball is dropped, then the first person to get to the ball gets possession.
- Touchdown is 6 points.
- After a touchdown, the team scored upon gets the ball at the middle of the field.

Fours
Equipment: Footballs
Group Size: 4 or more
Description:

- To start the game, one team is on offense and the other team is on defense.
- The offensive players consist of a quarterback and pass receivers.
- The defensive players consist of a pass rusher and pass defenders.
- The object of this activity is to see how far one team can get down the field in four downs.
- The pass receiver may only rush the quarterback after counting to three.
- After counting, the pass rusher may attempt to tag the quarterback.
- The quarterback may not run, but must pass the ball before s/he gets tagged.
- When a pass is completed, the offensive team moves to the spot of the completion and takes their next down from that spot. No player is allowed to run with the ball.
- After four downs, the offensive team marks the spot they reached with a cone and the teams switch roles.
- The new offensive team attempts to beat the distance set by the other offensive team.
- The team that is able to progress the farthest in four downs is awarded one point.
- The game is played to ten points.

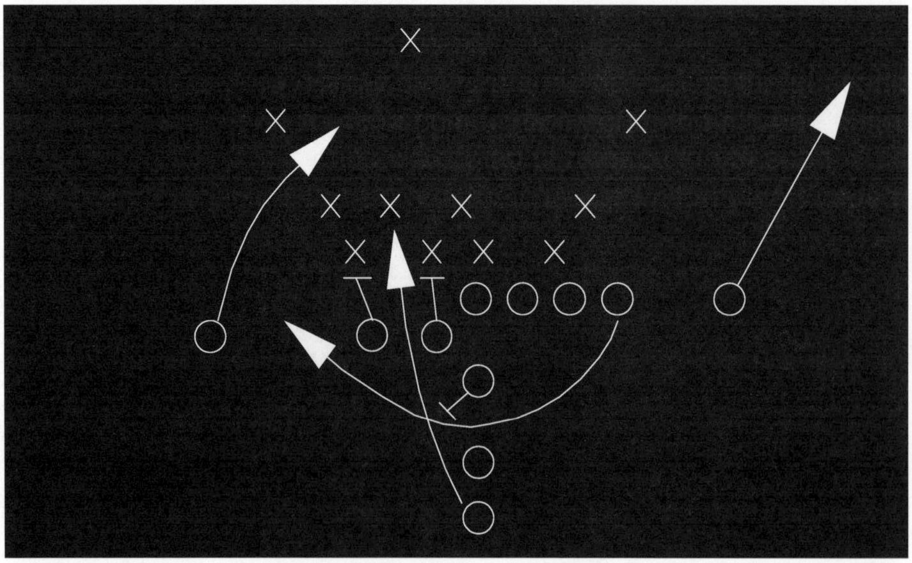

Football 21

Equipment: Footballs, pinnies, and end line markers

Group Size: Team of 5 to 6 students

Description:

- The offensive team consists of a quarterback and pass receivers.
- The defensive team consists of pass defenders and one pass rusher.
- The pass rusher must count slowly to three before s/he can rush the quarterback.
- The object of the game is to be the first team to score exactly twenty-one points.
- In order to score points, a pass must be completed.
- The point value of the pass is dependent upon the place at which the pass is caught.
- An incomplete pass is worth zero points.
- Start the game with a center snap to the quarterback.
- The pass receivers run out into the scoring area.
- The quarterback can pass to any of his/her receivers.
- After each pass, the offensive and defensive teams switch places.
- Each time a team returns to the offensive or defensive role, all team members must assume a different role; e.g., quarterback must become a receiver, pass rusher must become a pass defender.
- A team must score exactly twenty-one points.
- If a team has twenty points and the next pass is caught in the two-point area, the team loses all points and starts at zero.

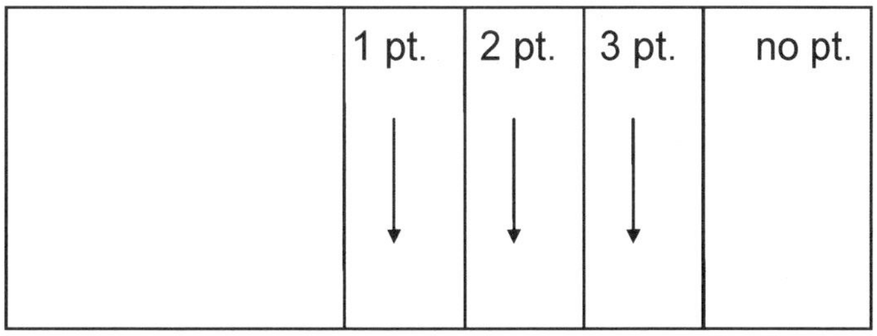

5 on 5 Football Game

Equipment: 1 Ball per game, flags

Group size: 5

Description:

- The game starts with a center snap at midfield.
- The team with the ball has 4 downs to make it to midfield.
- It they make it to midfield then they get an additional 4 downs to score.
- If the offensive team does not make it to midfield or score a touchdown in their four allotted downs, then the other team takes over at midfield.
- If the ball is run or passed across end line, that team scores 6 points.
- Play a 5 minute half, 1-minute conference time, and a 5 minute half.
- Rotate teams and play again.

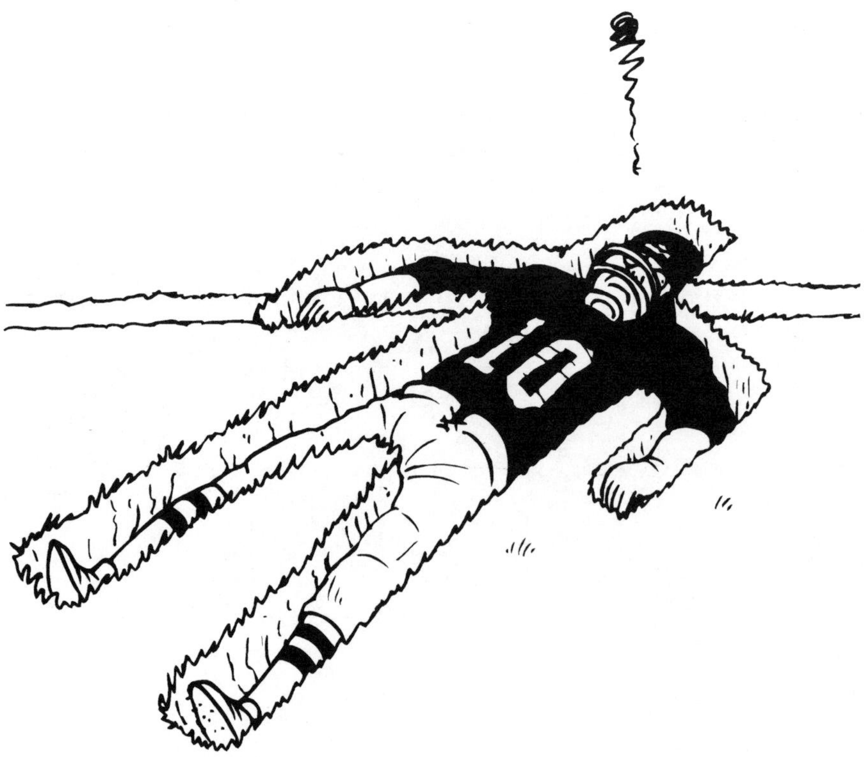

Hockey

Hockey

Hockey (Floor, Field)

Skill Progressions

1. Dribbling
2. Passing - push, drive or slap
3. Tackling
4. Shooting
5. Goal keeping
6. Offensive and defensive strategies

Ball Handling Activities

Stick Handling Suggestions

- Crossover dribbles
- Air dribble
- Stick Jumps
- Loose dribble
- Close dribble
- Zig-zag dribble
- Partner passing
- Partner shuffle passing
- Follow partner around the field

Skill Drills

Cross-Country Dribble

Equipment: 1 Ball and hockey stick per person, a designated or marked outdoor running course
Group Size: Individual
Description:

- Describe or explain the running course. Make the distance about a mile.
- Give the students a skill (close dribble, loose dribble, passing, etc). They work on the skill as they run the course.

Random Dribble

Equipment: Ball and hockey stick for every person
Group Size: Individual
Description:

- Each player has a partner ball and dribbles anywhere in the playing area.
- On a signal, the students should perform an immediate stick stop and do crossover dribble until the go signal is given.
- Dribbles should be close to the stick and under control.

Guard Your Own

Equipment: Sticks and pucks for all students
Group Size: Individual
Description:

- As many students as possible (safely) have pucks and sticks and are dribbling around a designated area. (May want to divide the group into several smaller groups).
- The object of the game is to protect your own puck while knocking as many other pucks out of the area in a designated amount of time.
- Once a student's puck is knocked away, then s/he should retrieve it and re-enter the game.

Passing Warm-up

Equipment: 1 Ball per pair, hockey sticks for each person
Group size: Pairs
Description:

- Partners stand 10 feet apart and try to make as many passes as possible in 30 seconds.
- At end of 30 seconds, the partners begin to jog and pass the ball to each other anywhere in the playing area for the next 30 seconds.
- Repeat sequence for 5 minutes

Gates

Equipment: Cones, 1 ball per pair
Group Size: Pairs
Description:

- Partners should set up their two cones about 2 steps apart somewhere in the playing area. The cones are the gates.
- One partner passes the ball through the gates.
- The other partner must receive and play the ball back through the gates within 2 touches.
- Play for 30 seconds.

Variations

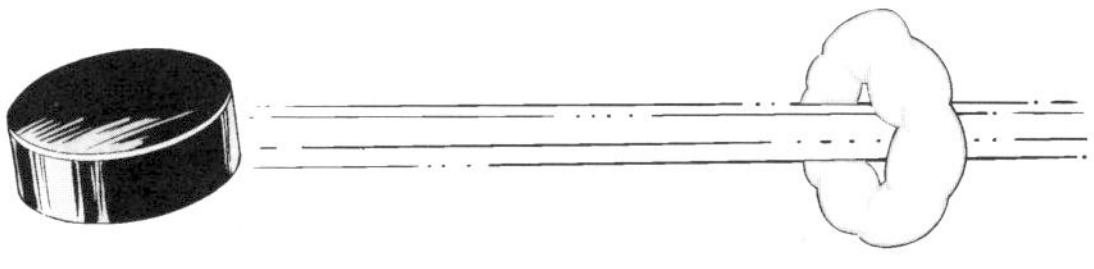

- Vary the distance away from gates
- Run from gate to gate

Shadow dribble

Equipment: Balls for every one
Group Size: Pairs
Description:

- One person stands behind the other one.
- The partner in the back attempts to follow the front person as that person dribbles anywhere in the playing area.
- Switch after 1 minute.

Center Jump Goal
Equipment: Ball and hockey stick for everyone
Group Size: Individual
Description:

- Place 4 goalies in the basketball center jump circle of the gym.
- The goalies attempt to keep all the balls out of the center jump circle.
- The rest of the class is dribbling and attempting to score by hitting the ball into the circle.
- Play 1-minute rounds and see which foursome can prevent the fewest scores.

The Race Track
Equipment: 1 Ball per group, hockey sticks, cones to mark off a circle
Group Size: Pairs
Description:

- Have one of the partners stand on the outside of the racetrack with a hockey ball.
- On signal, this person dribbles around the outside of the track while his/her partner is performing a hockey skill.
- When the dribbler returns home, the other person dribbles around the racetrack.
- Skills that can be performed on the inside of the track by the waiting partner include:
  1. Stationary cross-over dribble
  2. Scoops into a bucket
  3. Air dribble
  4. Jump over the hockey stick

200 Passes
Equipment: Sticks for all, 1 puck per pair
Group Size: Pairs
Description:

- Have partners face each other.
- On a signal, the partners begin passing the puck back and forth as quickly as possible.
- Have one line rotate up to a new partner every 15 seconds.
- The object is to get 200 passes before returning to the original partner.

3 Ball Keep Away
Equipment: 3 Hockey balls per field
Group Size: 5
Description:

- Use small grid fields.
- On a signal, players try to possess as many balls as possible for 1 minute.
- At the end of 1 minute, the team in possession of 2 balls wins that round.
- Play to 5 points and rotate teams.

Variations:

- Each player must hold the ball a minimum of 5 touches before passing. Reduce the number of touches to 2.

Snake

Equipment: One ball for every 3 people, stick for every student
Group Size: 3
Description:

- Middle player (B) starts with the ball. Player B must try to follow the head of the snake, Player A. Player C follows Player B.
- On a signal, B stops the ball and becomes the new head of the snake.
- Player A goes to the end and Player C has the ball in the middle.
- Encourage the head of the snake to move at different speeds, including stopping.
- Middle player must keep eyes up to see the head of snake.

Hockey Hunt

Equipment: Ball and hockey stick for all students, hockey sticks
Group Size: Pairs
Description:

- One of the partners should come into the center of the field (IT). His/her partner starts somewhere in the playing area.
- On a signal, both partners begin to dribble.
- The object is for the IT to find and tag partner. Once the partner has been tagged, s/he must do 10 crossover dribbles in place.
- The other partner dribbles away from the partner while s/he is doing the crossover dribble.
- The person doing crossover dribbles is now IT and chases his/her partner.

Monkey in the Middle

Equipment: 2 balls per group, sticks
Group size: 3
Description:

- One person starts in the middle of the other two persons.
- On signal, the middle person receives a pass from one of the outside people.
- After stopping the ball, the person quickly passes it back and turns around to receive the next ball from the other person.
- Go for 30 seconds and see which person can stop and pass the most balls.

Pass and Go
Equipment: Balls for 1/2 of the group, sticks for each person
Group Size: Groups of 8
Description:

- Within a 50x50 grid, half of the players should be on the inside of the grid without the balls. The remaining team members should be on the outside with balls.
- Inside players move around the grid freely, and receive a ball passed from the outside player.
- Change after 1 or 2 minutes.

Progression

- Return the ball with two touches
- Receive, do a short dribble and then return the ball.

Tackle Box
Equipment: Cones, 2 or 3 balls per group, sticks for each student
Group size: 4
Description:

- Cones should be used to designate a 10-yard by 5-yard box. This area is the Tackle Box.
- Select one student to be the defender of the Tackle Box.
- One at a time, the other three students attempt to dribble through the box without having the defender steal the ball.
- Switch defenders every minute.

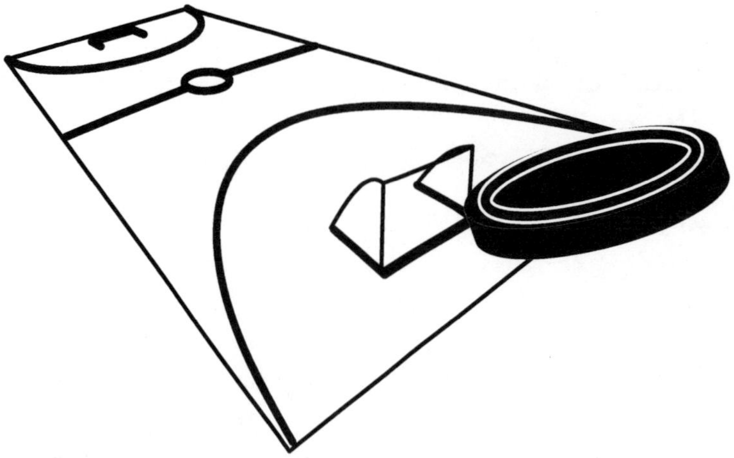

Hockey Hub
Equipment: Ball per person, sticks for each student
Group Size: 4
Description:

- Before class, the teacher should write down various hockey skills on index cards.
- These cards are placed in box in the center of the field (HUB).
- Group members take turns running to the HUB to retrieve a card.
- When the person returns to the group, the group members perform the skill(s) indicated on the card.
- After the group finishes the task, a new group member runs to the HUB and brings back a new card.
- Continue for 5 minutes.

Task examples

1. Place the hockey stick on ground. Jump back and forth over the stick 30 times.
2. With a partner, move across the field performing push passes.
3. Air dribble using one or all sides of hockey stick (try for 10 air dribbles without a miss).
4. Do 25 sit-ups with a partner while passing a hockey stick back and forth.
5. Invent three safe stretches using the hockey stick.
6. In a square, see how many consecutive push passes can be made in 30 seconds.
7. Zigzag dribble in and out of the cones.
8. Using a reverse stick, do 20 push passes to the partner.
9. Practice dodging the partner on his/her stick and non-stick side.

Race for the Goal
Equipment: Ball for every 2 students, sticks for each student
Group size: 2 teams
Description:

- The game starts with all players inside the center area, randomly dribbling a ball.
- The teacher calls out a team and those players must immediately dribble their ball toward their goal line. The other players leave their ball and play defense.
- Offense scores a point by dribbling in control over the end line. The defense can score a point by stealing the ball and dribbling it back to the center.

Team Pirates
Equipment: Hockey sticks and balls
Group size: Two teams
Description:

- Have one team wear pinnies.
- Each person on one team has hockey balls.
- The other team is trying to capture as many hockey balls as possible from the other team in 30 seconds. The offense may not try to steal the ball back.
- Once a person has his/her hockey ball stolen, that person must run to the side line and get a hockey ball and dribble around the outside of the area until a new game begins.

Protect A Pin
Equipment: Cone per pair, sticks and ball
Group Size: Pairs
Description:

- Have one of the partners stand in front of pin. That person guards the pin.
- The other person tries to hit the cone with the ball. Persons with the ball can dribble to any cone and attempt to hit any person's cone.
- Have the person dribbling count the number of cones hit in 1 minute. Switch with the partner and then have the partner try to hit cones.
- After both have gone, have them try to beat their score.

Lead-up Games

1 on 1 Cone Hockey
Equipment: Cones and 1 ball per 2 students
Group size: Pairs
Description:

- Have each pair place 2 cones a set distance apart (40').
- The object is to hit the opposite person's cone with the hockey ball.
- One partner begins with the ball and attempts to hit the partner's cone.
- The person may attempt to steal the ball at anytime to become the offensive player.
- Each pair starts at either cone with the ball at one of the cones.
- Play 1-minute games and rotate partners.

2 on 2 Cone Ball
Equipment: 1 ball per group, sticks for all, cones
Group size: Pairs
Description:

- Have one pair challenge another pair to a game.
- Each pair should put a cone about 20 feet apart.
- The object is to hit the opposing team's cone with the ball.
- This game is similar to the 1 on 1 cone ball game.
- Play 2-minute games and rotate to a new team.

Two Sided Goal
Equipment: 2 cones per field, one ball per field
Group size: Pairs
Description:

- Set up small grid fields with 2 cones (as goal) in the middle of each field.
- Have pairs find another pair to compete against.
- On a signal, the teams try to score through either side of the goal.
- Play 2-minute games and rotate.

3 Line Hockey
Equipment: 2 Cones per field, 3 balls per field, pinnies
Group size: 9
Description:

- Divide the group into teams of 9 and place them in 3 rows in the playing area (3 goalies, 3 defenders and 3 forwards).
- The 3 forwards on each team have a ball.
- On a signal, the 3 forwards face off and attempt to score the ball. When they score, they bring the ball over to the teacher. This process allows the teacher to keep score and controls the tempo of the game.
- When all balls have been scored, goalies rotate to defenders, defenders to forwards and forwards to goalies.

Variation

- The object is to try and score as many points as possible in 2 minutes.

8 on 8 with corner goals
Equipment: 16 cones per field, 2 to 3 balls per field, pinnies
Group size: 8
Description:

- Set up 10-yard squares in each corner of small grid fields. These act as goals.
- A goal is scored when the ball is passed into the square and then out to a teammate.
- Each team can attack any of the four goals. However, once a team has scored at one goal, they may not score at that goal again until they score at one of the other 3 goals.

Variations:

- Play with 2 or 3 balls.
- Allow players to receive a pass and then dribble out to score a goal.

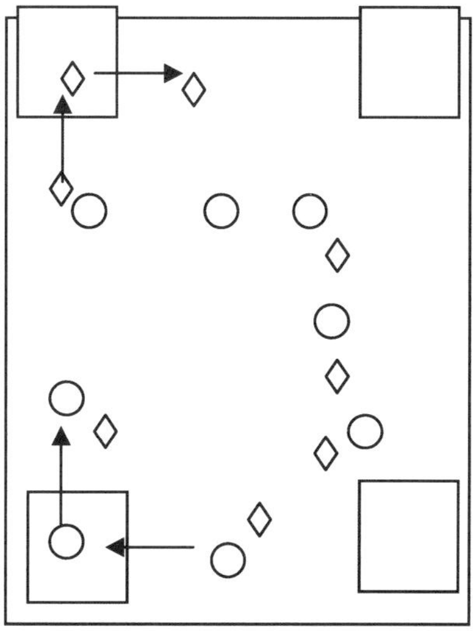

Ultimate Floor Hockey
Equipment: Pinnies, 1 or 2 balls per game,
Group Size: 5 to 7 per team
Description:

- The game is played like Ultimate Frisbee. The object is to score a goal by stopping a ball behind the goal line. The ball must be stopped without any noticeable rebounding from stick.
- The ball is put in play with a face off.
- After each score, the defending team takes the ball out from behind the end line.

Additional Scoring Rules

1. Passed to a teammate and stopped on the end line (2 points).
2. Hit between goals (3 points).

6 Goal Field Hockey or Floor Hockey

Equipment: Ball for every group (color code the ball), goal area, 5 colored flags for each group, pinnies.

Group Size: 4

Description:

- Assign each team a different color (red, blue, green, black, yellow, white).
- The object is for the teams to score a goal in every other team's goal.
- If there are 4 in a group, 1 person is the defense and the other 3 are on offense. No goalies.
- Once they score, they take one of the color flags from a cone located behind the goal area.
- Once a team has collected all 5 colors, reset and change positions.

5 on 5 Game

Equipment: 1 Ball per field, pinnies, and goal markers

Group size: 5

Description:

- Regular hockey rules.
- The object is to try to score a goal by shooting the ball between the cone markers.

Lacrosse

Lacrosse

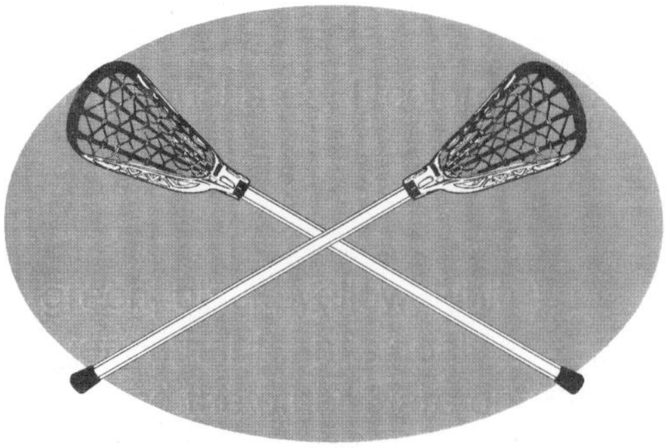

Skill Progression

1. Cradling
2. Catching
3. Throwing
4. Defensive position
5. Shooting
6. Offensive and defensive strategies

Basic Ball Handling Activities

- Cradling without a ball and no movement
- Cradle without ball and move
- Cradle with ball and without movement
- Cradle with ball and with movement
- Cradle, toss and catch to self, cradle
- Cradle, toss, let ball bounce one time, catch, cradle
- Cradle, roll out ground, scoop, cradle
- Rock the Baby
- Cradle the ball
- Cradle and toss to self
- Cradle and toss to partner - stationary
- Cradle and toss to partner while moving
- Scoops, cradles, drops and repeat to self
- Scoops, cradles, drops and partner picks up
- Dodging around cones

Skill Drills

Throwing and Catching Progression
Equipment: Ball and stick for every person
Group Size: Pairs
Description:

- Have one person underhand toss ball to partner (Stick side). Partner should catch (reach and give) the ball and then toss it back to the partner.
- Have one person underhand toss ball to partner (Nonstick side). Partner should catch (reach and give) the ball and then toss it back to the partner.
- Throw ball to wall and catch own throw. (Practice shovel pass, overhand pass and side arm passes).
- Throw and catch between partners.
- Throw and catch on the run.

London Bridge

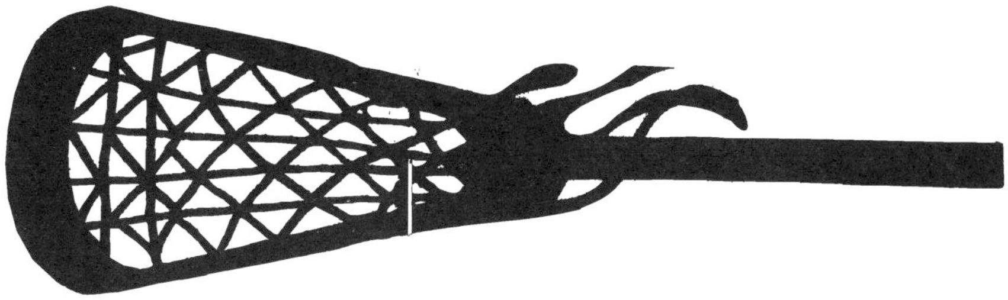

Equipment: Sticks for all students, ball for every two

Group size: Pairs

Description:

- Have one player in each pair place ball beside his/her foot about 12 inches away.
- Have player extend his/her arm from the shoulder over the ball and let his/her stick hang down toward the ground so that it forms a bridge over the ball.
- Partner without the ball starts 10 yards from the bridge and accelerates under the bridge to perform a ground ball pick-up.
- As soon as the ball is in the stick, s/he accelerates and begins a cradle.
- After about 3 cradles, s/he drops ball and sets up a bridge for partner.

Mass Pass

- Students should get a partner and arrange themselves like diagram below. A variety of stick handling skills can be developed. The person on the inside of the square has a ball. On a signal, the person passes to the partner and then the partner passes the ball back to the partner. The person on the outside of the square must move across the circle to find a new person to receive a pass from. This process continues for 30 seconds. Switch the inside and outside groups. Examples follow:

  Overhand pass
  Scoops
  Shovel pass
  Sidearm pass

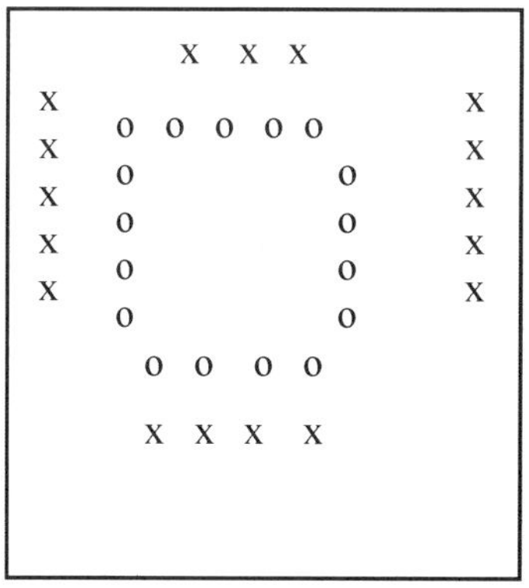

Numbers Pass

Equipment: Ball and stick for each person

Group size: 6

Description:

- Each person should be given a number (1 - 6).
- Practice the passing 1 time before moving the group. Have each person pass the ball to the next highest number (e.g., 1 to 2, 3 to 4, 6 to 1).
- After an initial practice, each person should begin cradling the ball around a designated space.
- On a signal, they must pass to the next highest number.
- Time the groups and see if they can improve the time that it takes to complete the task.

Variations

- Perform the task without talking.

Lollipop Passing Drill
Equipment: Sticks for all, 1 ball per group
Group size: Pairs
Description:

- Have the person with the ball perform an over the shoulder lob pass to the partner.
- The partner runs forward to catch the pass. As soon as the first tosser passes the ball, s/he runs forward to receive a pass from his/her partner.
- Continue this process back and forth across a field.

Bear at the End of the Bridge
Equipment: Sticks for all students, ball for every two
Group size: 3
Description:

- Have one player in each pair place the ball beside his/her foot about 12 inches away.
- Have that player extend his/her arm from the shoulder over the ball and let his/her stick hang down toward the ground so that it forms a bridge over the ball.
- The partner without the ball starts 10 yards from the bridge and accelerates under the bridge to perform a ground ball pick-up.
- The third person is positioned about 5 yards from the bridge and is the bear. The player performing the pickup must control the ball right away and dodge the bear.
- The bear may reach out and try to prevent the ball carrier from picking up ball or cradling, but s/he may not move feet.
- The person, who is cradling runs ahead, drops the ball and becomes the new bear. The bear becomes the bridge and the bridge is the ball carrier.

Monkey in the Middle
Equipment: 1 Ball per group, sticks
Group size: 3
Description:

- Player 1 and player 2 stand facing each other about 10 yards apart.
- As player 1 passes the ball to player 2, defender (monkey) stands one step in front of player 1 to block the pass.
- If pass is blocked, s/he carries ball to where 3 is standing and then 3 tries to block.
- If unsuccessful, s/he must circle player 1 and jog to player 3 and try to block the pass.

Pass and Go
Equipment: Balls for 1/2 of the group, sticks for each person
Group Size: Groups of 8
Description:

- Within a 50x50 grid, half of the players should be on the inside of the grid without the balls. The remaining team members should be on the outside with balls.
- The inside players move around the grid freely, and receive a ball passed from the outside player.
- Change after 1 or 2 minutes.

Progression

- Receive, do a short cradle and then return.

Cougars on the Chase
Equipment: Sticks for all, ball per group
Group size: 4
Description:

- Have two players stand about 15 or 20 feet apart and begin to toss the ball back and forth to each other.
- The other two players are 5 yards to the side and directly in the center of the two players.
- As the ball leaves the stick, one of the players in the waiting line attempts to run in and intercept the ball.
- Change the position of the players after 1 minute.

Lacrosse Hub
Equipment: Ball per person
Group Size: 4
Description:

- Before class, the teacher should write down various lacrosse skills on index cards.
- These cards are placed in box in the center of the field (HUB).
- Group members take turns running to the HUB to retrieve a card.
- When the person returns to the group, the group members perform the skill(s) indicated on the card.
- After the group finishes the task, a new group member runs the HUB and brings back a new card.
- Continue for 5 minutes.

Task examples

1. Place lacrosse stick on ground. Jump back and forth over your stick 30 times.
2. With a partner, move across the field performing passes.
3. Do 25 sit-ups with a partner while passing lacrosse stick back and forth.
4. Invent three safe stretches using your lacrosse stick.
5. In a square, see how many consecutive passes can be made in 30 seconds.
6. Zigzag run and cradle in and out of the cones.
7. Using a shovel pass, do 20 passes as quickly as possible with a partner.
8. Practice the pull, roll and dodge with a partner.

English Channel
Equipment: 1 Ball per group, cones, sticks
Group Size: 4
Description:

- Mark off space about 10 yards by 20 yards with cones.
- One of the group members has the ball and stick.
- Another player has no stick. The attacker runs through the channel while the defender tries to maintain proper body position and works on footwork.
- Rotate defender after the person has defended all 3 offensive players.
- Second time around, have the defender start halfway across the channel and toss the ball to the first person. As soon as the pass is made, run and close the gap.

The Race Track
Equipment: 1 Ball per group, hockey sticks, cones to mark off a circle
Group Size: Pairs
Description:

- Have one of the partners stand on the outside of the racetrack with a hockey ball.
- On a signal, this person cradles around the outside of the track while his/her partner is performing a lacrosse skill.
- When dribbler returns home, the other person cradles around the racetrack.
- Skills that can be performed on the inside of the track by waiting the partner include:
    1. Passes to self
    2. Scoops into a bucket
    3. Cradle
    4. Jump over lacrosse stick

Lead-up Games

Keep Away
Equipment: 1 Ball per game, pinnies, sticks
Group Size: 4
Description:

- The object of the game is to make as many consecutive passes as possible without losing control to the opposite team.
- Each defensive player must stay with a designated opponent.
- If the ball is intercepted, give it back to the offensive team and have them begin counting again.
- Go for 1 minute and then give possession to the opposite team.

2 Team Keep Away
Equipment: 2 Balls per field, pinnies, sticks
Group size: 6
Description:

- Use 2 small grid fields per group.
- One grid should contain the following configuration – 4 red players and 2 blue players. The other grid should have 2 red players and 4 blue players.
- The four players are the offensive players and try to make 5 consecutive passes (1 point).
- The two defensive players try to steal the ball and make two consecutive passes (1 point).
- Play 2-minute games and rotate people on the fields.

3 Ball Keep Away
Equipment: 3 Balls per field
Group Size: 5
Description:

- Use small grid fields. Each game has 3 balls.
- On a signal, the players try to possess as many balls as possible for 1 minute.
- At the end of 1 minute, the team in possession of 2 balls wins that round.
- Play to 5 points and rotate teams.

Variation:

- Each player must hold the ball a minimum of 5 seconds before passing.

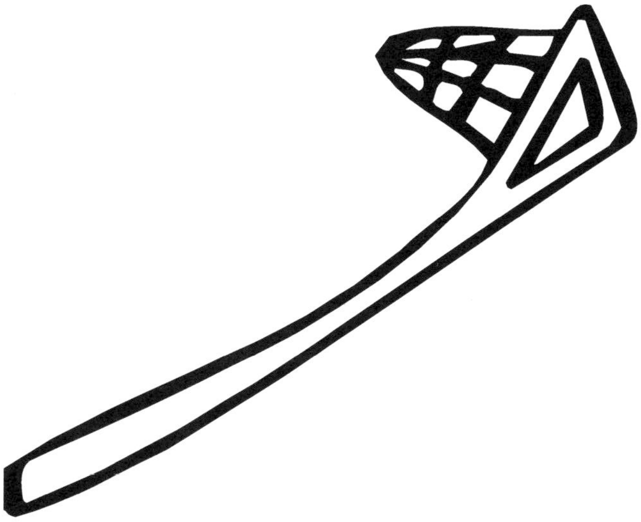

2 on 2 Cone Ball
Equipment: 1 Ball per group, sticks for all, cones
Group size: Pairs
Description:

- Have one pair challenge another pair to a game.
- Cones should be placed about 20 feet apart.
- The object is to hit the opposing team's cone with the ball.
- Play 2-minute games and rotate to a new team.

8 on 8 with Corner Goals
Equipment: 16 Cones per field, 2 to 3 balls per field, pinnies
Group size: 8
Description:

- Set up 10-yard squares in each corner of small grid fields. These act as goals.
- A goal is scored when the ball is passed into the square and then out to a teammate.
- Each team can attack any of the four goals. However, once a team has scored at one goal, they may not score at that goal again until they score at one of the other 3 goals.

Variations:

- Play with 2 or 3 balls.
- Allow players to receive a pass and then cradle out to score a goal.

Ultimate Lacrosse
Equipment: 1 Ball per group, cones to mark end lines, pinnies, sticks
Group size: 4
Description:

- Use small field grids.
- The players may not run with the ball. They must pass and may pivot.
- The defender of the ball carrier must stay one stick's distance away and may only block a pass.
- To score a goal, the ball must be caught behind the end line.
- After a goal, the ball is given to a defensive player who takes it from behind the end line.

5 on 5 Game
Equipment: 1 Ball per field, pinnies, goal markers
Group size: 5
Description:

- Regular lacrosse rules. The object is to try and score a goal by shooting the ball between cone markers.
- No goalies.

Soccer

Soccer

Skill Progressions

1. Dribbling - inside and outside of foot
2. Passing - inside, outside and instep
3. Trapping
4. Volleying
5. Tackling
6. Goalkeeping
7. Offensive and defensive strategies

Basic Ball Handling Activities

Basic Ball Handling Series

- Quick feet taps on top of the ball
- Ball jumps
- Roll over the ball (both feet)
- Knee volleys
- Foot volleys
- Foot volleys with partner (moving backward)
- 2 Touch passes with a partner

Soccer Fitness

Equipment: Ball per pair
Group Size: Pairs
Description:

- The pairs begin in a center area. Each student has a soccer ball. They perform each activity for 30 seconds.
    1. Inside foot dribble to the sideline and back to the center circle.
    2. Toe taps on top of the ball.
    3. Grapevine dribble with rear foot to the sideline and back to circle.
    4. Crunches with the ball between feet.
    5. Toe taps clockwise and counter-clockwise.
    6. Face the outside of circle. Punt and retrieve the ball. Dribble back with the outside of the foot dribble.
    7. Jump over the ball side to side.
    8. Jump over the ball front and back.
    9. Jump over the ball crisscross.
    10. One partner dribbles clockwise on the outside of circle, the other partner dribbles counterclockwise on the inside of the circle.
    11. Soccer juggle with body parts.
    12. Push-ups with hands on the ball.
    13. One partner chases the other and trying pass ball and hit the partner's soccer ball.

Skill Drills

Walk-the-Dog

Equipment: Balls for every student or every 2 students
Group Size: Individual or pairs
Description:

- Have students perform a close dribble around a given area.
- If students are working in partners, they should dribble and pass around a defined area.

Pinball Soccer

Equipment: Empty tennis can or bowling pin and soccer ball per group
Group Size: Groups of 4
Description:

- Put a pin up and have one of the students in the group stand in front of it.
- The object is for the other three to form a circle around the pin and move the ball in order to knock pin over.
- Go for a set amount of time and then switch the middle person.

Bridges and Tunnels

Equipment: Soccer balls or nerf balls
Group Size: Partners
Description:

- Divide the class in half. Half of the students have a ball and the other half form a tunnel by standing in a stride position anywhere in a specified area.
- The students with the balls dribble to the players who are forming a tunnel and pass the ball between their legs. When a ball passes through a tunnel, the person forming the tunnel must drop into a crab position. When another ball passes under a person in a crab position, he/she once again becomes a tunnel. Players with the ball count the number of tunnels and crabs they pass the ball through.
- Time the activity for one minute. Have the students repeat this activity in the same positions. Challenge the dribblers to get to five more tunnels than they did the first time.
- Switch places and have the tunnels be the dribblers and the dribblers be the tunnels.
- A variation of this activity is to see how long it takes each half of the class to close all of the tunnels. A tunnel is closed when five balls have been passed through it.
- When a tunnel closes, the tunnel player holds the up position of a push-up. Try to see which half of the class can close the tunnels the quickest.

Speedaway Lifts
Equipment: 1 Ball per person
Group size: Pairs
Description:

- Practice individually and in pairs lifting the ball to self and partner.
- 1 foot and 2 feet lifts.

Variations:

- Compete with partner to see how many 2 feet lifts they can get in 30 seconds.
- Each person has a ball. Face the partner. Roll the balls at same time .
- See how many consecutive rolls and lifts can be made in 30 seconds.

Pass and Go
Equipment: Balls for 1/2 of the group
Group Size: Groups of 8
Description:

- Within a 50x50 grid have half the players (4) on the inside of the grid without balls and 4 on the outside with balls.
- The inside players move around the grid freely and receive a ball from the outside players and return it as quickly as they can.

Progression

- Touch the ball twice before returning it (Stop it and pass it).
- Receive the ball with the outside of the foot and then the inside of the foot.
- Receive, do a short dribble and then return.

Snake
Equipment: Balls for every 3 people
Group Size: 3
Description:

- The middle player (B) starts with the ball. Player B must try to follow the head of the snake, Player A. Player C follows Player B.
- On a signal, B steps on the ball and becomes the new head of the snake.
- Player A goes to the end and Player C has the ball in the middle.
- Encourage the head of the snake to move at different speeds, including stopping.
- The middle player must keep eyes up to see the head of snake.
- Encourage the use of many different surfaces of the feet in contact with the ball.

Cross-Country Dribble
Equipment: 1 Ball per person, a designated or marked outdoor running course
Group Size: Individual
Description:

- Give each student a ball.
- Describe or explain the running course.
- Give students a skill (close dribble, loose dribble, heading, passing, etc.) to perform as they run the course.
- Go for a set amount of time.

Gates
Equipment: Cones, 1 ball per pair
Group Size: Pairs
Description:

- Two players per gate (two cones about 2 steps apart).
- The player with the ball passes the ball through the gates.
- The partner must receive and play the ball back through the gates within two touches.
- Play for 30-second trials.

Variations

- Vary the distance away from gates.
- Run from gate to gate.
- Receive with one foot and play it back with the other.

3 Ball Keep Away
Equipment: 3 Soccer balls per field
Group Size: 5
Description:

- Use small grid fields and 3 soccer balls per field.
- On a signal, the players try to possess as many balls as possible for one minute.
- At the end of one minute, the team in possession of 2 balls wins that round.
- Play to 5 points and rotate teams.

Variations:

- Each player must hold the ball a minimum of 5 touches before passing. Reduce the number of touches to 2.
- Each player may only use his or her dominant foot.

Corner Passing

Equipment: 4 Balls per field
Group Size: 4
Description:

- Have 3 teams per grid. Each player on Team 1 is located at a corners of the field.
- Team 2 is the offense. Team 3 is defense.
- The offense must get free and receive a ball from the players in the corners and play it back without losing possession.
- After 1 or 2 minutes, rotate positions on the field (Team 1 goes to defense, Team 3 goes to offense and Team 2 goes to corners).

Points to stress

- Take the defender away from the passer to create a space to receive.
- Receive sideways on and not straight on.

Variations

- Must return the pass to a different corner person each time.

Gauntlet

Equipment: One ball per 2 people
Group Size: Pairs
Description:

- Arrange the class in 2 parallel lines. Partners should be facing each other.
- Players in Line X should have the ball.
- Each player starts the activity with their partner and receives a pass and then moves up to next person. The last person in the line must run to the end of the line to get a pass.
- When students have returned to the original partner, switch places.

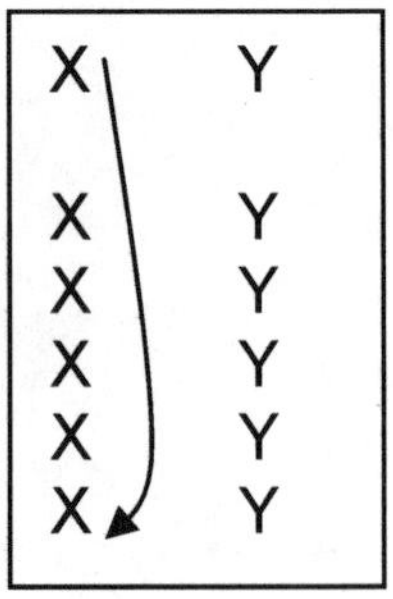

Variations:

- Receive with the inside and pass with the outside of the foot.
- Receive with the instep and pass back with the instep.
- Receive with the chest and pass back with foot.

Race for the Goal

Equipment: Ball every 2 students.
Group size: Split the group into 2 teams
Description:

- The game starts with all players inside the center area randomly dribbling the ball.
- The teacher calls out a team and those players must immediately dribble their ball toward their goal line. The other players leave their ball and play defense.
- Offense scores a point by dribbling in control over the end line. The defense can score a point by stealing the ball and dribbling it back to the center.

1 on 1 Basic
Equipment: 4 or 5 Balls per field
Group Size: 3 to 5 people per field
Description:

- Use small grid fields. 2 players challenge each other on the inside of the grid.
- Players on the outside of the grid pass a new ball to players when the ball is kicked out.
- The person with the ball attempts to dribble the ball across the opposite end line. If the person succeeds, that person stays and immediately turns around and goes back against a new defender.
- If the defender takes the ball away, the defender takes the ball to the end line.
- S/he is now on offense ready to face a new defender.
- Keep going for 2 minutes. Reinforce the following points:
  1. Always try to face the defender and shield the ball sideways on.
  2. Don't dodge too early or too late.

Soccer Spiderball
Equipment: 6 Cones per field, spots to mark shooting spot, balls for half class
Group size: Groups of 12
Description:

- The object is to see how quickly all of the cones of each team can be knocked down.
- On a signal, the shooters begin kicking the balls from behind the boundary line (10 yards from cones).
- The retrievers must remain behind the cones. They need to get the balls back to the shooters as fast as possible.
- When a team knocks all the cones down, they yell, "stop." Switch retrievers and shooters and play again.

2 Team Keep Away
Equipment: 2 Balls per field, pinnies
Group size: 6
Description:

- Use 2 small grid fields per group.
- One grid should contain the configuration of 4 red players and 2 blue players. The other grid should have 2 red players and 4 blue players.
- The four players are the offensive players and try to make 5 consecutive passes (1 point).
- The 2 defensive players try to steal the ball and make two consecutive passes (1 point).
- Play 2-minute games and rotate teams to a new field.

Foxes and Hunters
Equipment: 1 Ball for every other student (use nerf balls if possible for safety)
Group size: 8
Description:

- Play on a small grid field. Put half the group on the inside (foxes) of the grid. The other half is on the outside (hunters) of grid with the balls.
- On a signal, the hunters dribble into the grid and try to hit the foxes below the knee.
- If a fox is hit, the fox must perform 10 push-ups.
- After 1 minute, switch roles.

Emphasize

- Discourage long range shooting.
- Try faking and then shooting.
- Work in pairs to get foxes cornered.

Transfer Boxes
Equipment: 1 Ball per field
Group Size: 8 per field (4 on each team)
Description:

- Set up two grids together with a cone separating the two areas.
- Have one grid with 4 players on 2 players. The other grid has the remaining two players.
- On a signal, the team with 4 players plays keep away from the team with 2.
- If the defending team steals the ball, they try to play it to the other box where the other two teammates are waiting.
- When the pass is made, the two players who stole the ball quickly follow their pass for support.
- The other team then sends 2 players in to the other area to steal the ball back.
- Play continues to transfer from one box to the other.
- If the ball goes out of bounds, use a throw in to put ball in play.

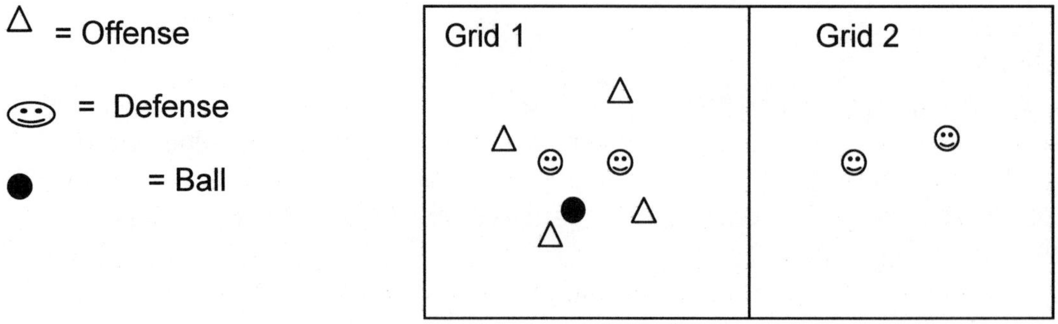

Scramble
Equipment: 3 Balls per ten students
Group size: Individual
Description

- Three to five goals are set up and have 3 balls for every 10 students in class.
- The people with the balls try to score on the goals.
- There are no teams, thus players function independently.
- Players without a ball attempt to gain possession of the ball and in so doing, prevent others from scoring.
- If a player scores a goal or misses, play continues.
- If a goalie catches the ball or stops a shot, s/he trades places with the player who shot it.
- If the ball is taken away from a player, then the player, who took it away, tries to score.

Pass 200
Equipment: 1 Ball pair
Group Size: Pairs
Description:

- Have partners stand across from each other.
- On a signal, students instep kick with the person across from them counting the total number of kicks.
- Every 15 seconds, blow the whistle and move one line, 1 person to the right.
- The goal is to achieve 200 passes before they return to the original partner.

Two Sided Goal
Equipment: 2 Cones per field, one ball per field
Group size: Pairs
Description:

- Set up small grid fields with 2 cones (as goal) in the middle of each field.
- Have pairs find another pair to compete against.
- On a signal, the teams try to score through either side of the goal.
- Play 2-minute games and rotate.

Pass and Defend
Equipment: 1 Ball per group
Group size: 3
Description:

- Player A rolls the ball to player C.
- Player A then immediately challenges player C and tries to win the ball back.
- Player C must complete a pass to Player B.
- If C completes a pass, C gets the ball and rolls to Player B.
- If A wins the ball back, s/he continues to roll.
- Play for a set amount of points (10 points and rotate threesomes).

Numbers Pass
Equipment: Ball for each person
Group size: 6
Description:

- Each person should be given a number (1-6).
- Practice the passing 1 time before moving the group. Have each person pass the ball to the next highest number (e.g., 1 to 2, 3 to 4, 6 to 1).
- After an initial practice, each person should begin dribbling the ball around a designated space.
- On a signal, they must pass to the next highest number.
- Time the groups and see if they can improve the time that it takes to complete the task.

Variations

- 2 Touch passing
- Perform the task without talking

Goalie Warm-Up
Equipment: 3 Balls per group, 3 cones per group
Group size: 4
Description:

- Set up a triangular goal with cones 12 feet apart.
- Players A, B, C each have a ball.
- Player D starts at one of the cones.
- Player A rolls the ball towards the opposite cone. Player D runs, slides or dives to stop the ball and returns the ball to A.
- Player B then rolls the ball to the next cone. Player D moves to stop the ball.
- Go for 90 seconds and switch goalies.

Pin Defend
Equipment: 1 Cone per group, 1 ball per group
Group size: 4
Description:

- Set one cone up for each group. Make sure there is enough space between each group.
- With 4 in a group, have 1 person stand by the pin (goalie).
- The object of the activity is for the 3 other people to pass and move the ball around in order to knock the pin over.
- Use a time limit (1 minute as goalie) and then switch goalies.

Knock Out

Equipment: 1 Ball per person
Group size: 8 to 10 in a grid
Description:

- Use small grid fields.
- The object of the game is for each student to protect his/her own ball while trying to kick the other player's soccer ball out of the grid.
- If a student's ball is kicked out, that student retrieves it, does five push-ups and returns to game.
- Play for a set amount of time. Mix players on the grids.

Numbers Up Keep Away

Equipment: 1 Ball per group
Group size: 3 to 5
Description:

- Use a small grid field.
- The game is a basic keep away game. One team tries to keep the ball from the other team.
- The offensive team should always have more players than the defensive team. (3v1, 5v2, 3v2, etc).

Variations:

- Whoever loses the ball trades with the defensive player.
- Play for a set amount of time and see how many passes can be made among offensive players.

Soccer Fun

Equipment: Soccer ball
Group Size: 2 equal groups
Description:

- The fitness game is a competition between two groups.
- Group A is in the center of playing area. Each person must do a selected exercise (push-ups, sit-ups, line jumps, etc.) One person from Group A is running around the group as many time as s/he can before the Group B finishes its task.
- Group B is chasing a ball thrown or punted by the teacher. When they get to the ball, they complete an assigned task (pass the ball to each person, pass over head, etc.) When they are done, A stops running and counting.
- Group B must quickly come into the center. Group A now chases the ball.
- Go for a set time.

Bubba's Keeper

Equipment: 1 Ball per group, 4 cones per group
Group Size: Pairs
Description:

- Set up cones to mark off 2 goal areas about 20 feet apart.
- Keeper A tries to throws the ball into Keeper B's goal area and visa versa.
- The first keeper to score wins.
- Rotate to a new field.

Variation

- Give both keepers a ball.

Escape

Equipment: 1 Ball per group
Group Size: 7 per group
Description:

- Divide the group into 5 offensive players and 2 defensive players.
- The 5 offensive players must make 10 passes. (1 point per 10 passes).
- The 2 defensive players are trying to get the ball and take (dribble with control) the ball out of the field (1 point).
- Play to 3 points and rotate positions.

1v1v1

Equipment: 1 Ball per group
Group size: 3
Description:

- Play on small grid fields.
- Player C starts on the end line and dribbles into zone 1 and tries to get past defender A.
- If A steals the ball, then A tries to dribble past C and over the end line.
- If C manages to get past A, C continues through Zone 2 (free zone) and into Zone 3 and tries to dribble past defender B to get to the end line.
- If B steals the ball, s/he goes to zone 2 and challenges player A.

Variations:

- Allow defender A to chase C into Zone 2.

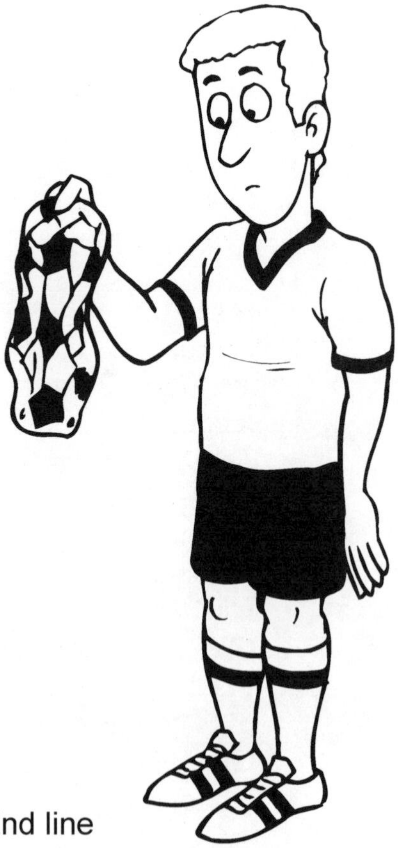

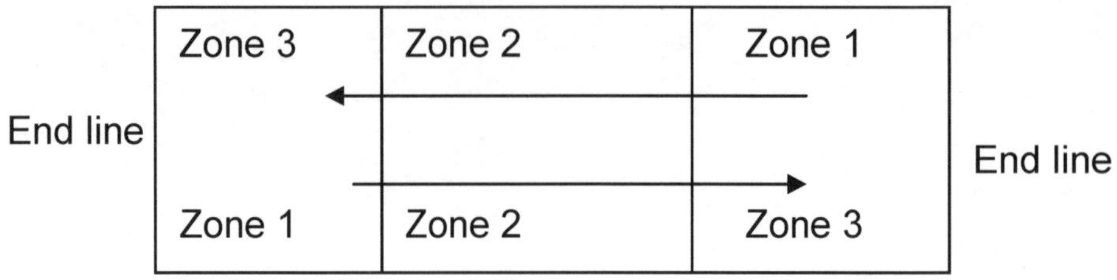

Lead-up Games

All-Out Soccer

Equipment: Nerf balls or trainer soccer balls (enough for 3/4 of the class to have a ball), pinnies for teams, two boxes or containers for each field.
Group Size: Teams of 8
Description:

- Make enough fields for all teams of 8 to play (e.g., 64 students you need 4 fields - 2 teams of 8 on each field). Mark goals with cones about 6 feet apart.
- Each team begins the game on its own side of the playing field. Divide up the balls evenly. Each team should have about 5 balls.
- All soccer rules apply, except there are no goalies.
- After scoring a goal, the person who scores must pick up the ball used to score the goal and place it in the box.
- Team A will place their balls in the box next to their goal and Team B will place their balls in the box next to their goal.
- After the ball is placed in the box, the person who scored the goal must run to the box of the other team. They take a ball out of their own team's box and start playing again.
- If there are no balls, they wait for one.
- Have a way for student's to make a mark on the box each time s/he scores.

1 on 1 Cone Soccer

Equipment: Cones and 1 ball per 2 students
Group size: Pairs
Description:

- Have each pair place 2 cones a set distance apart (40').
- Each pair starts at either cone with the ball at one of the cones.
- The object is to hit the opposite person's cone with the soccer ball.
- Play 1-minute games and rotate pairs.

Triangle Goal Game

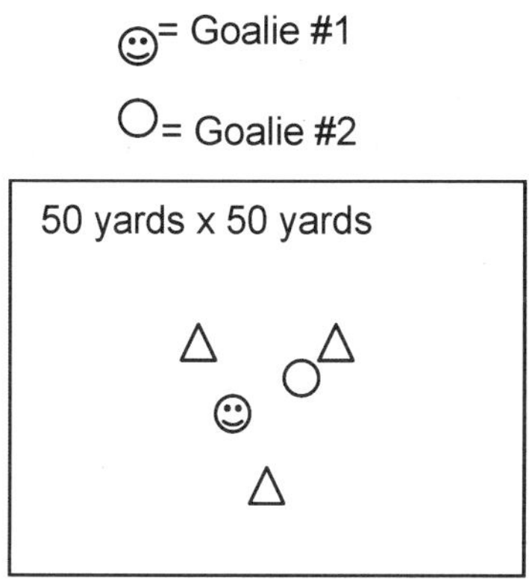

Equipment: 3 Cones for every field and 2 balls
Group Size: Teams of 6 to 8
Description:

- Set up a triangular goal in the middle of a 50x50 grid. Put the goal inside a 20-foot diameter circle.
- Both teams try to score through any one of the three sides of the triangular goal.
- If the goalie catches the ball, the offensive team must take the ball outside the grid before they try to score again.
- Switch goalkeepers every 2 minutes.

Speed Box

Equipment: Nerf balls or trainer soccer balls (enough for 3/4 of the class to have a ball), pinnies for teams, two boxes or containers for each field.

Group Size: Teams of 8

Description:

- Make enough fields for all teams of 8 to play (e.g., 64 students you need 4 fields - 2 teams of 8 on each field). Mark goals with boxes or containers (1 for each team).
- Each team begins the game on its own side of the playing field. Divide up the balls evenly so that each team has about 5 balls.
- All soccer rules apply, except there are no goalies.
- A goal is scored by lifting the ball into the opponent's container.
- After scoring a goal, the person who scored must run back to his/her own container and get a ball out of the box and try to score again.
- If there are no balls, the student should wait for one.

Ultimate Speed Soccer

Equipment: Pinnies, 1 or 2 balls per game,

Group Size: 5 to 7 per team

Description:

- The game is played like Ultimate Frisbee. The object is to score a goal by catching the ball behind the goal line.
- The ball is put in play with a center kick. If the ball is on the ground, the players must follow soccer rules. If the players convert the ball to an aerial ball, the ball may be passed (no running) to teammates.
- After each score, have the defending team take a free kick.

Additional Scoring Rules

- Use a goal and allow a throw over the end line or a kick into the goal.

6 on 6 Speedaway

Equipment: 1 Ball per game, pinnies
Group size: 6
Description:

- Use small fields (30x20yd or 40x25yd with goals 8 feet apart).
- The game is started with a push-kick backwards.
- The object of the game is to advance the ball down the field by kicking, dribbling, running or throwing.
- Scoring occurs by:
  1. Touchdown – throw or the run ball across the end line (2 points).
  2. Goal – Kick the ball through the goals (3 points).
  3. Field Goal – drop kick the ball over goal posts (4 points).
  4. If a player is running with the ball, the opposing team may tag the person. If the runner is tagged, the runner must stop and pass the ball at that point.
  5. If the ball touches the ground, it must be played as soccer ball (no hands). Players may lift the ball and turn it into an aerial ball that may be run or thrown.
  6. If the ball goes out over the sidelines or end line (without scoring a goal), the opposing player must use a 2-handed throw in.
  7. After a goal, the ball is started at the half field mark with a push-kick.

Soccer Ladder

Equipment: 1 Ball per field and 2 cones per field
Group Size: Pairs
Description:

- Place cones 10 yards apart to form one playing field for one game. Each playing field is 10 yards away from the next one.
- These cones are the goals. Set up as many fields as necessary to get all students active.
- The game is played one-on-one. Players defend their own cones while trying to attack and score at an opponent's goal.
- Games are limited to 2 minutes. At the end of 2 minutes, successful players move up the ladder and unsuccessful players move down the ladder.
- If the score is tied at the end of the time, player in control of the ball is winner.

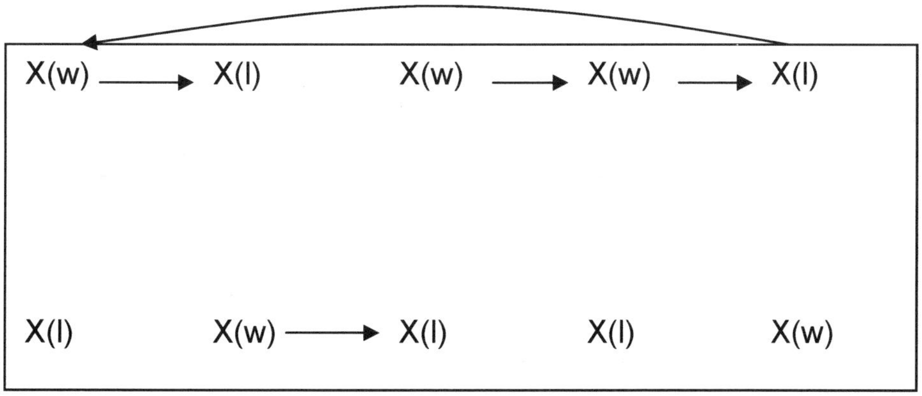

Winners move up to next the cone and losers stay. At the top end, the winner stays and the loser goes to first cone.

War

Equipment: 3 Balls for each field, goal on one end of the field, cones to mark field in 3 areas

Group size: 10

Description:

- Divide the group into defenders (3) and the goalie. The other 6 players are attackers.
- Three attackers stand on the end line. Each has a ball. The object is to dribble through all three zones and score on the goalie.
- Two defenders are in zone 1, one defender in zone 2 and the goalie is in zone 3.
- The defenders try to get the ball out of their zone (in control – can't be kicked).
- As soon as the attack person has moved into the next zone, the next attacker can begin.
- Attackers go through 3 times and then switch with a defender or goalie.

Variation:

- Might want to leave zone 2 as a free zone, so when the attacker gets there, the person has time to rest.

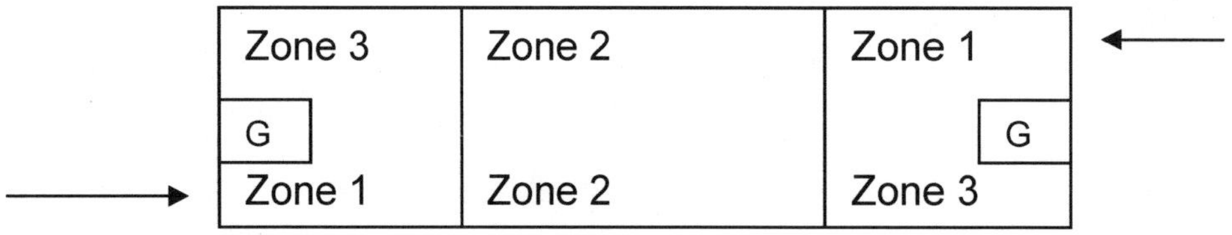

8 on 8 with Corner Goals

Equipment: 16 Cones per field, 2 to 3 balls per field, pinnies

Group size: 8

Description:

- Set up 10-yard squares in each corner of small grid fields. These act as goals.
- A goal is scored when the ball is passed into the square and then out to a teammate.
- Each team can attack any of the four goals. However, once a team has scored at one goal, they may not score at that goal again until they have scored at one of the other three goals.

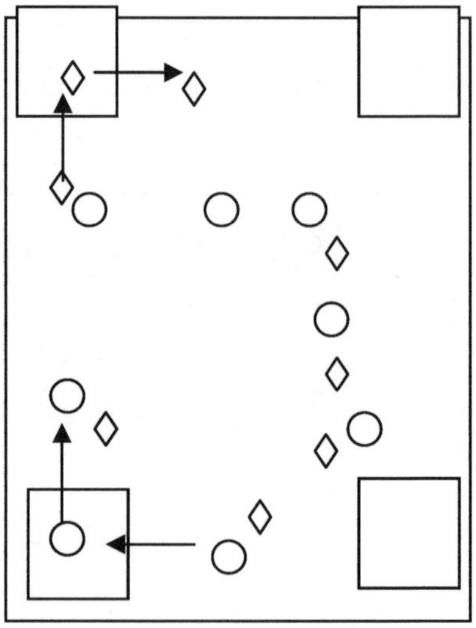

Variations:

- Play with 2 or 3 balls.
- Allow players to receive a pass and then dribble out to score a goal.

Softball

Softball

Skill Progressions

1. Throwing and catching
2. Fielding
3. Batting
4. Pitching
5. Base running
6. Offensive and defensive strategies

Basic Ball Handling Activities

- Throwing and catching to partner
- Ground balls with partner
- Fly balls with partner
- Pepper with partner - one bunting the other fielding and tossing back

Catch 200
Equipment: Enough throwing objects for every other person, cones
Group Size: Pairs
Description:

- Set up the cones in a straight line (1 cone for every 2 people).
- Have each pair get a throwing object and then the person with the ball go stands by the cone. The partner stands about 15' from him/her.
- On a signal, the pair begins to throw and catch as quickly as possible.
- After 15 seconds have everyone not at a cone move to the right one person.
- The object is to achieve 200 catches before person returns to his/her home station.

Workback
Equipment: Balls for pair
Group Size: Pairs
Description:

- Each pair should have a ball and stand about 5' apart.
- On a signal, the pair begins to throw and catch. With every successful catch, the person who caught the ball takes a step backward.
- If the pair drops the ball, the pair begins again at the centerline.
- Establish a distance the pairs cannot exceed.

Skill Drills

Sesame Street Fielding

Equipment: 1 Ball for each pair (write a number on each ball with 4 different color magic markers – green, red, blue, black)
Group Size: Pairs
Description:

- Each pair should get a ball and face the partner standing about 10' away.
- All pairs should be facing each other as diagramed below.
- On a signal, one player rolls a grounder to the other partner.
- The partner fields the ball and tells partner what number was written on the ball.
- Have pairs leave the ball and move to the next station to the right. Keep going through the line until they are back to home position.

X	O
X	O
X	O
X	O
X	O

Bullpen Softball

Equipment: Bases
Group Size: 3
Description:

- Teams should each have a home base (poly spot).
- One member of each team begins a lap around the bases. If that student hears any of the following calls, he/she stops and performs the task.

Fly ball:	Freeze and then sprint to home base.
Grounder:	Defensive stance and side slide to home base.
Pinch Hitter:	The person running freezes, and the next person in line runs out and completes the lap hooked at the elbows.
World Series:	Run to give the teacher a high 5 and finish the lap.
Double Play:	The runner sits down and the other members of the Bullpen comes and carries him/her back to the starting point.

Crash and Burn

Equipment: 1 Tennis ball per pair
Group size: Pairs
Description:

- Make sure each pair has plenty of space.
- One player throws the ball up while the other person calls, "mine" or "yours".
- If a ball is dropped or the wrong player catches the ball, then the person committing the error gets a E (ERROR).
- First person to spell error loses.

4-Player Softball

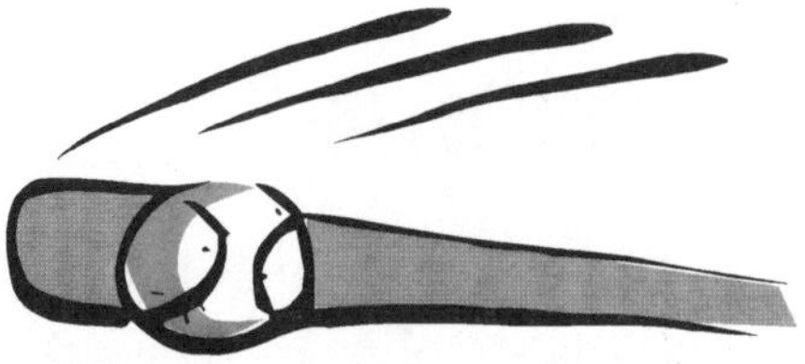

Equipment: 1 Pillo polo stick or whiffle bat per group, 1 ball (nerf or wiffle) per group.
Group size: 4 people per group.
Description:

- Assign positions of catcher, pitcher, batter, and fielder to the people in each group.
- The batter gets one pitch to hit.
- As soon as the ball is hit, everyone rotates as quickly as possible (see diagram).
- Once the pitcher is in place, she/he can pitch, even if the batter is not ready.
- Keep going for a set amount of time.

Set-up:

```
      c          c          c
   b        b          b

      p          p          p

      f          f          f
```

C= catcher
B= batter
P= pitcher
F= fielder

Mass Pass

- Students should get a partner and arrange themselves like diagram below. A variety of ball handling skills can be developed. The person on the inside of the square has a ball. On a signal, the person passes to the partner and then the partner passes the ball back. The person on the outside of the square must move across the circle to find a new person to receive a pass from. This process continues for 30 seconds. Change the inside and outside positions and repeat. Examples follow:

```
        x   x   x
x   o  o  o  o  o    x
x   o            o   x
x   o            o   x
x   o            o   x
x   o            o   x
      o  o   o  o

        x   x   x   x
```

  Pop ups
  Grounders
  Bunting

Side Slide with 1 Ball
Equipment: 1 Ball per pair
Group Size: Pairs
Description:

- Partners face each other about 10' apart.
- On a signal, both players begin shuffling clockwise in a circle while rolling the ball to each other.
- Reverse directions after 30 seconds.

Variation

- Use 2 balls to increase the challenge.

Running Bases
Equipment: 1 Ball per group, 2 cones or poly spots for every group
Group size: 2
Description:

- Have one pair challenge another pair. One pair is the base runners and the other pair is the throwers.
- The object is for the runners to exchange places with each other as many times as they can without being tagged out.
- The tossers begin throwing the ball. The runners must run on every third throw.
- Two runners cannot occupy the same base.
- Go for 2 minutes before changing tossers and runners or change every 3 outs.
- Rotate teams after a few minutes.

Zig Zag Run
Equipment: 1 Ball per group
Group Size: 4
Description:

- Have each group form 2 lines (2 facing 2).
- Designate a set distance for the group to travel.
- On a signal, the last person in the line tosses the ball to the person across from him/her and then runs to the front of the line.
- The object is to see how many trips the group can take in 2 minutes.

1 on 3 Softball
Equipment: 2 Bases, 1 bat and one ball per game
Group size: 4
Description:

- The set-up for this game is two bases (home and one about 15 yards away).
- The players take one of 4 positions - outfield, pitcher, batter or catcher.
- The batter hits the ball into the field and begins running from base to base.
- S/he continues to run until the fielders relay the ball into the catcher who tags home plate. All fielders must touch the ball before the relay to catcher.
- The batter scores a run for every base touched.
- The players then rotate, to assume a new position and a new batter is up.
- Fielders may not run with the ball.
- A ball caught in the air is still in play and a foul ball is a strike.

Batting Stations
Equipment: Tennis balls, cones, bats, balls
Group size: 3
Description:
Station #1 - Soft Tosses - One person soft toss the ball, one person bats and one person fields. Switch places after 5 pitches.
Station #2 - Drop Drills - Use some type of backstop and a bucket or box. Have one player hold the ball at shoulder height and drop it straight down into the strike zone. The batter must see the ball and react fast enough to hit it. Drill teaches batter to take their hands straight to the ball. Have the player dropping the ball, drop them at different times so the batter does not start to cheat. The third person fields the balls. Switch places after 5 drops.
Station #3 - Barrier Drills - Have the batter stand one bat's length from a barrier (net, fence, etc). The batter takes a normal swing. If s/he hits the barrier, the person is unlocking her/his elbows before his/her shoulders and getting too wide on the swing. Have each person take 25 swings.
Station #4 - Tee Drills - Hitting balls off the T (cone).
Station #5 - Superball Drills - Get 3 old basketballs and take most of the air out of them. Put the basketball on the T. The students hit the ball off the T.
Please note: Teach the students how to stand when soft tossing for safety. Make sure stations are spaced far enough apart.

- If the class is inside, an interesting variation is to create batting cages out of folding mats.
- Set mats every 4 to 5 feet across the gym. In each cage, put a basket of 4 to 5 foam softballs, a T and whiffle ball bat.
- Have some kind of mark for non-batting people to stand behind for safety.
- Have music to mark retrieval and batting. When music is on, the person in the cage is hitting and may not leave the cage until the music stops.
- When the music stops, the batter retrieves the balls and the next person gets ready to hit.

Overtake Base
Equipment: Bases
Group size: 6
Description:

- Put one team on second base and the other team at home.
- On signal, the first person in each line runs the bases until s/he gets back and tags the next runner.
- This continues until one team has run all the bases.

Boundary Softball
Equipment: Softball, bat, cones
Group Size: Two equal teams
Description:

- Before the game begins, mark out a playing area similar to the one diagrammed below.
- The batting team lines up across the field. The fielding team spreads out anywhere in the fielding area.
- To begin the game, the pitcher pitches the ball to the first batter.
- If the batter misses the ball, s/he passes the bat to the next person in line.
- If that person misses the ball, s/he passes the bat to the next person in line.
- This process continues until someone hits the ball.
- If no one in the line hits the ball, the batting team gets zero points and the fielding team and batting team change places.
- When a batter does hit the ball, the entire team must run across the field to the other boundary line.
- The fielding team must field the ball and then attempt to tag as many players as possible by touching them with the ball.
- Fielders may run to tag runners or throw the ball to other fielders who can tag the runners. Runners who are tagged must freeze until all of the runners have either made it to the other boundary line or have been tagged.
- Each tagged player counts as one point for the fielding team.
- Switch sides after every run.

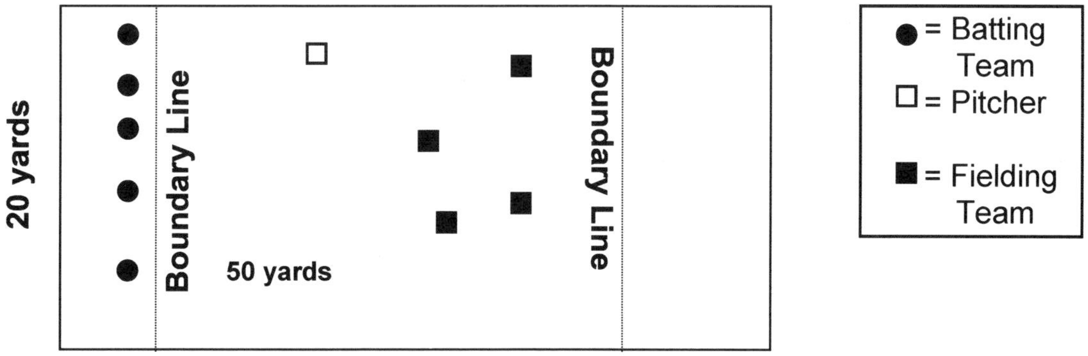

Go or NO
Equipment: None
Group size: Individual
Description:

- Have the students line up on a line facing the direction they will run.
- Mark a running distance that is about the length of a base path.
- The object of the activity is to simulate base running demands.
- The teacher gives the student a game situation. The players decide whether to run or not to run.

Examples

1. "Pop-up, he catches it (he drops it)."
2. "A ground ball."
3. "A wild pitch – catcher blocks it."
4. "Two outs and it's a pop up."
5. "A wild pitch – gets by the catcher."

Pepper
Equipment: 1 Ball and bat per group
Group Size: 4
Description:

- One batter and 3 fielders per field.
- One of the fielders tosses the ball to the batter who hits it back lightly.
- If a player fields it cleanly, s/he immediately tosses it back to the batter.
- Continue for 30 seconds. Rotate the batters and the fielders.

3 Ball Pitching
Equipment: 3 Balls per pair
Group Size: Pairs
Description:

- In pairs, one person has 1 ball and the other person has 2 balls.
- The person with 2 balls throws a pitch to the other person.
- The receiving player must receive the ball and pitch one back.
- The reason for 3 balls is to have no waiting or if one is missed.
- Throw 100 pitches between the pair.

3-2-1

Equipment: 3 Balls per group, cones or poly spots to mark bases
Group size: 4
Description:

- Have one group as the fielding team. The other team is the running team.
- Place 3 balls equal distance apart about ¾'s of the way from third to home.
- Have one runner on home plate and have one member of the fielding team at third and one at second base.
- On a signal, the runner must reach second base before the third base person throws all 3 balls to the second base person.
- All throws must reach the second baseman.
- If the runner gets there before the throws or if there is a bad throw, the running team gets 1 point.
- If the throws beat the runner, then the fielding team gets a point.
- After the first runner, quickly reposition the balls, new fielders and new runner.
- Play 2-minute rounds. Switch the running and fielding teams.

500

Equipment: 1 Ball and bat per group
Group Size: 4
Description:

- One batter and 3 fielders per field.
- The batter hits the ball to the fielders.
- The fielders get points depending upon how the ball is caught (fly ball = 100, 1 bounce = 50 points, ground ball = 25 points)
- Whoever gets 500 points gets to be the new batter.
- Go for 1 or 2 minutes and then have the groups switch batters if no one has gotten to 500.

Hitting Coach

Equipment: 7 to 10 Balls, 1 bat and container per group
Group Size: 6
Description:

- Have one group of 6 challenge another group.
- Each group should designate their hitting coach.
- Each team lines up about 40' from their hitting coach.
- The box should be half way between the coach and the team and to the side.
- The hitting coach hits a ground ball, a player fields the ball and runs the ball to bucket.
- When all balls are used, the team switches the hitting coach. Balls are brought to the new coach and play begins again.
- The first team to complete all members as hitting coach is the winner.

Base Drill
Equipment: 1 Tennis ball and 2 cones per group
Group size: 4
Description:

- One person is the tosser. The other 3 are the runners.
- The runners start at one cone. The tosser starts a short distance in front of the runners.
- The tosser takes the tennis ball and holds it at eye level.
- The first runner must keep one foot at the cone until the tosser lets go of the ball.
- As ball is dropped on a board or flat surface, the runner leaves the base and attempts to catch the ball before it bounces off the wood.
- Have each person take a turn as the tosser.
- The distance for this drill is determined by skill level. Start out close and then begin to move the students back as their skill improves.

Softball Darts
Equipment: 1 Ball per group, targets on wall or fence
Group Size: Pairs
Description:

- The object is to work on the underhand pitching motion by aiming at the targets. (Center = 10 pts, 2nd ring = 8 pts., 3rd = 6 pts., 4th = 4 pts.)
- Each person challenges the another person.
- One person pitches 5 balls and then adds up score.
- The partner tries to beat that score.
- Play 3 innings (5 balls each). Total the score in each inning.

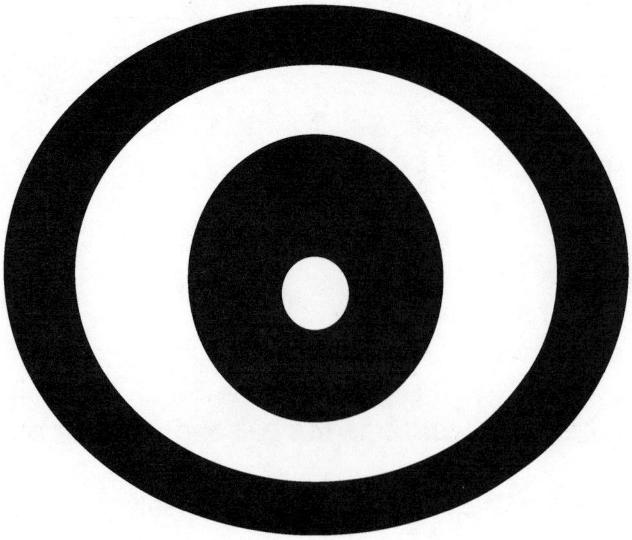

Lead-up Games

Fitness Softball

Equipment: Box and 5 nerf balls
Group Size: Two equal teams
Description:

- One team is at bat. The other team is in the field.
- Located next to home base is a box. In the box are 5 balls.
- The first person to bat goes to the box, picks up one ball. S/he throws the ball into the field and begins to run the bases. Balls must be thrown into the field of play.
- As soon as the first batter rounds first base, the next batter takes another ball from the box and throws it.
- The fielders must retrieve the balls and put them back in the box.
- The fielding team must never let the box be empty.
- The batting team is trying to throw the ball and run bases as fast as possible in order to score runs.
- After everyone has batted, the teams switch places.

Scoring:

- If the fielding team fails to keep at least one ball in the box, the batting team gets a point.
- If the fielding team keeps at least one ball in box until the end of inning, then the fielding team gets a point.
- At the end of each complete inning, take a ball away.
- During the second inning, the teams are playing with only 4 balls in the box.
- Third inning, the box only has 3 balls. Do not go below 3 balls.

Triangle Ball

Equipment: 1 Tennis ball per group, 3 cones per group
Group Size: 6
Description:

- Have each group of 6 set out their cones in a triangular formation.
- Players divide into 2 teams. One batting team and one fielding team.
- Batters do not hit the ball, but throw it.
- In order for the batter to run, s/he must throw the ball so that it bounces in the triangular area.
- If the ball lands outside the area, then the batter is out.
- If the ball is bounced in bounds, the batter must run to the bases made by the cones.
- Fielders try to field the ball and tag the base or the runner.
- After three outs, the batting team becomes the fielding team.

Variation

- A challenging variation is to use a z-ball instead of a tennis ball.

21

Equipment: 1 Softball, bat per group (May want to have batting T's available for some students who can not fungo bat).

Group size: 4

Description:

- Have one student be the batter and the other 3 are fielders.
- The batter self tosses a ball and hits the ball to the fielding members.
- If a fielder catches the ball on a fly, then s/he gets 3 points. Catching the ball on one bounces results in 2 points. Catching a grounder is worth 1 point.
- The person who gets 21 first becomes the batter (Must get 21 exactly).
- Some groups may have difficulty getting to 21, so every 4 minutes have the students rotate batters and fielders.

Home Run Derby

Equipment: 1 Softball, bat per group

Group size: Pairs

Description:

- Have each pair challenge another pair.
- 1 pair bats and the other pair pitches and fields the balls.
- The object is to hit the ball (on a fly) into a designated area. Each time a team does that, they get 2 points. If the ball goes into the area on 1 bounce, they get 1 point.
- Any other hit is an out.
- Each team gets 8 outs.
- Play for 5 minutes and then rotate to a new team.

Babe Ruth Ball

Equipment: 1 Ball, bat, 1 home plate marker and 4 cones per group

Group size: 6

Description:

- Have each group set up the field in three zones (left, right and center).
- The team members assume the following positions, the pitcher, catcher, batter and 3 fielders.
- The batter calls out the field to which s/he intends to hit.
- The pitcher pitches the ball.
- The batter remains in that position as long as s/he can hit the ball to the "called" field.
- The batter may not call out the same field twice in a row.
- The batter gets one swing.
- If batter does not hit to the "called" field, then all players rotate.
- Rotation is: batter to right field, right field to center field, center field to left field, left field to pitcher, pitcher to catcher and catcher to batter.

2 on 2 Cone Ball
Equipment: 1 Ball, 1 bat, and 2 cones per group
Group Size: Pairs
Description:

- Teams should find another pair to challenge.
- Put cones about 40' apart.
- The object is to run from the starting to the other cone and back to the starting cone before the fielding team can hit the cone immediately in front of the runner with the ball.
- The batting team can self toss ball or use a T to hit the ball.
- Once the batter hits the ball, s/he must run to the opposite base. S/he can stay there if s/he beats the ball to the base. However s/he must leave after the partner hits the ball.
- The runner is out if the ball beats the runner to base or is caught on a fly.
- Change batting and fielding teams after 3 outs.
- Rotate teams after 5 minutes.

Snake Softball
Equipment: Softball, bat, and four bases
Group Size: Two equal teams
Description:

- The game is played like regular softball with the following exceptions.
- When the batter hits the ball, everyone on the batting team must form a single file line behind the batter (connect at the waist) and run the bases as a connected unit.
- The fielding team must field the ball and then throw it in the correct sequence (pitcher=1, catcher=2, 1st=3, 2nd=4, 3rd=5, SS=6, LF=7, CF=8, RF=9).
- If the batting team gets everyone across home plate before the ball is thrown to every one on the fielding team, the batting team scores one point.
- If the fielding team throws the ball to everyone in the correct sequence, then the batting team has one out.
- Switch batting and fielding teams after three outs.

Scrub Ball
Equipment: 1 Ball, 1 bat, bases per group
Group Size: 6
Description:

- The infield consists of just one base and home plate.
- There are no teams in scrub ball, just positions.
- The positions go in order from batter #1 to batter #2, catcher, pitcher, baseman, fielder.
- Each player plays for him/herself, but batters often have to work together to get each other around bases.
- Outs are made in the same manner as softball.
- If a batter is out, all players move forward one position and the batter becomes the fielder.
- The other batter stays where s/he is and plays with a new teammate.
- Players keep track of the number of runs they score individually.

3 Team Scrub Ball
Equipment: 1 Ball, 1 bat, bases per game
Group size: 2
Description:
- This is a team variation of scrub ball.
- On each field, there should be 3 pairs (1 pair is batting, 1 pair is the pitcher and catcher and 1 pair is the fielders).
- The infield consists of just one base and home plate.
- The batting teams are given two outs. The other teams must work together to get the batting team out.
- When the batting team has two outs, the players rotate as a unit; the batters become the fielder and baseman, the baseman and fielder become the pitcher and catcher, and pitcher and catcher become the batters.

Duck Soup Softball
Equipment: 1 Ball, 1 bat, bases per game
Group size: 2 teams
Description:
- One team is the batting team. The other team is the fielding team.
- Each inning the fielding or batting team is required to do something unique
  1. First inning - batting team runs bases starting at third base.
  2. Second inning - fielding team starts lying on their back and gets up when the ball is hit.
  3. Third inning - all fielders must clap three times before they can throw the ball.
  4. Fourth inning - all batters must run as pairs.

Aerobic Softball
Equipment: 1 Bat, ball and bases per game
Group size: 5
Description:

- Batting team must be 20 yards away from plate in batting order.
- One pitch per batter.
- Hit, miss, foul, fair, the batter runs to first base and tries to go as far as possible (may stop at any base).
- The fielding team tries to get the runner out in the normal fashion.
- If the player is safe, s/he stays on the base. If out (pop up, tag out, etc.), s/he runs to the end of the batting order.
- When the play is over, all fielders rotate. At this time, the next batter runs the 20 yards to home plate to bat and the fielding players move up (P to C, C to 1st, 1st to Short, Short to Outfield 1, Outfield 1 to Outfield 2, Outfield 2 to P).
- 3 outs and switch.

5 Person Derby Ball
Equipment: 1 Ball, 1 bat, bases per game
Group size: 5
Description:

- This game is played on a small field with only 3 bases (home, 2nd and 3rd).
- One team is up to bat. The other team is in the field.
- The fielding team must have a pitcher, catcher, and 3 fielders.
- The object is to score as many runs as possible.

Rules

- A batter only gets 2 pitches.
- A ball that is caught is an out.
- The ball must land in the defined area.
- Once the ball is hit, the runner goes from 2nd to 3rd to home.
- In order to get the batters out, the fielding team can catch the ball on the fly or tag the base before the runner gets there.
- Play 3 outs and switch batting and fielding teams.

Alley Ball

Equipment: Softball bats, 16” softballs, area markers

Group Size: 4 to 5 per team

Description:

- Mark off the field as shown below. After each batter, the outfield team rotates positions.
- The object is to score as many runs as possible in a set number of innings.
- Game rules are similar to regular softball except:
  1. Each batter gets only two pitches. Pitches are made underhand and must cross the batting area.
  2. Once the ball is hit, the batter must run from home to the outfield base and back home. The batter may stop at the outbase if s/he cannot make it back home without being tagged out.
  3. All batters hit and the sides change.
  4. If the ball is hit outside the alley, the teams automatically change offensive and defensive positions.

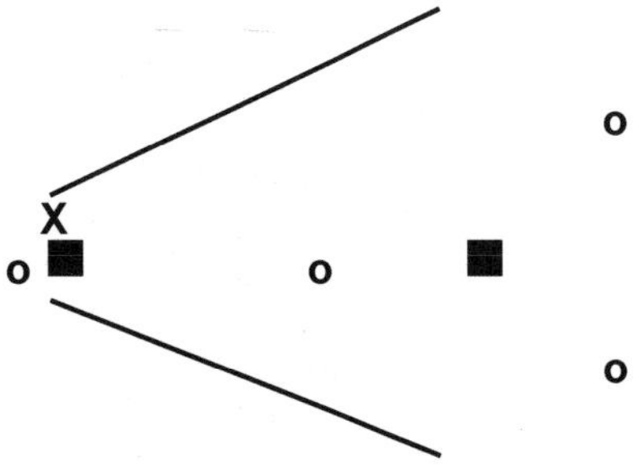

Team Handball

Team Handball

Team Handball

Skill Progression

- Passing (overhand, wrist, bounce)
- Dribbling and running combinations
- Shooting (set shots, jump shots)
- Defensive positioning
- Goalkeeping
- Offensive and defensive strategies

Basic Ball Handling Activities

Basic Ball Handling Series

- Overhand pass to partner
- Overhand pass to partner while moving
- Wrist pass to partner using both right and left hands
- Wrist pass to partner while moving
- Catch 5 out of 10, 6 out of 10, 7 out of 10, 8 out of 10, 9 out of 10 and 10 out of 10 balls thrown against the wall
- Catch 5 out of 10, 6 out of 10, 7 out of 10, 8 out of 10, 9 out of 10 and 10 out of 10 bounce passes thrown from partner
- Jump pass to partner
- Walk and dribble the full length of gym
- Skip and dribble to half court
- Run and dribble with right hand to half court and then run and dribble with left hand to end line
- Shoot high set shots
- Shoot low set shots
- Shoot bounce shots
- Shoot high jump shots
- Shoot low jump shots
- Shoot bounce jump shots
- Catch ball from goalkeeper, dribble the length of court and shoot a goal

Random Partner Passing
Equipment: Balls for every 2 students
Group Size: Pairs
Description:

- Each player has a partner and a ball. The partners move and pass anywhere in the playing area.
- Students are encouraged to vary distances and types of passes (bounce, overhand, etc)
- Variation: Each pair has two balls and throws and catches both simultaneously.

Passing Numbers
Equipment: One ball per group
Group Size: Groups of 5
Description:

- Each player in the group is given a number (1-5).
- On 'Go', the groups begin jogging anywhere around a designated area tossing and catching the ball to group members.
- On the whistle, the group needs to pass the ball from 1 –5 (in sequence) as quickly as possible.
- To make it more challenging, have two balls being passed by the group.

The Clock
Equipment: 1 Ball per group, cones
Group Size: Groups of 5
Description:

- Two groups will challenge each other. One group is standing on the inside of the circle and the other group is on the outside of the circle.
- On a signal, the outside group runs around the outside of the ring, while the inside group performs various passes.
- Go for a set amount of time and see how many times the entire group can get completely around the circle.
- Switch places and have the inside group run and the outside group pass.

10 Passes
Equipment: Ball per pair
Group Size: Groups of 5
Description:

- Use a small area as a court.
- The object is to make 10 consecutive passes without having the other team intercept the ball. If the ball is dropped or held for more than 3 seconds, the group must start back at zero. If the ball is intercepted, the other team begins to try to make 10 passes.
- If a team gets 10 passes, they get one point.
- Play games to 3 or 5 and rotate the teams.

Catch 200
Equipment: Ball per pair
Group Size: Pairs
Description:

- Have partners stand across from each other.
- On a signal, the students throw and catch with the person across from them counting the total number of catches.
- Every 15 seconds, blow the whistle. One line moves 1 person to the right.
- The goal is to achieve 200 catches before they return to the original partner.

Mirrors
Equipment: Ball per pair
Group Size: Pairs
Description:

- The first student runs a set distance, turns to partner, receives a pass, then back pedals to start.
- As soon as the partner gets back to start, the other one goes.
- Continue this pattern for a set amount of time.

Partner Pass Tag
Equipment: Ball per pair, music with intervals of silence
Group Size: Pairs
Description:

- Each pair should find a safe starting position anywhere in the playing area.
- When the music begins, the pair begins to pass the ball back and forth with each other.
- When the music stops, whoever has the ball, chases the person without the ball (walking only).
- If the person is tagged, the chaser puts the ball down. The new chaser picks it up and does 10 dribbles and then chases the other person.
- When the music comes back on, they begin passing again.

Hit and Run Warm-up
Equipment: Numbers from 1-40, team handballs
Group Size: Pairs
Description:

- Post numbers 1-40 in random order anywhere around the gym.
- Have one partner stand by one of the numbers without a basketball.
- The other partner stands in the center of the gym with a team handball performing ball-handling skills.
- When music comes on, the student by the number runs back and tags partner and begins doing ball handling.
- The other partner runs to the next highest number (start at 7 - s/he goes to 8).
- Go for 1 minute and see if they can beat the number they have completed on the next set.

Skill Drills

Hoop It Up
Equipment: 1 Hoop, polyspot or tape mark per group, one nerf ball per group
Group Size: 4
Description:

- Put half of the group on one side of the playing area facing the other two individuals in the group.
- Put a hoop or poly spot in front of the group (enough distance to allow running toward the ball and three steps following the catch).
- The person with the ball takes three steps and on the last step puts opposing foot from throwing arm into the hoop. S/he makes a throw to opposite line. The person should back pedal to the end of his or her own line.
- The person receiving should run toward the ball to catch it. Back up and take 3 steps to their hoop.
- After they get the idea of 3 steps, have them run to receive the ball take three steps and end up with foot in the hoop. Jog to the opposite line to continue.

Partner Piston Passing
Equipment: 1 Ball per group, cones
Group size: Groups of 4
Description:

- Put half of the group on one side of the playing area facing the other two individuals in the group. The groups are about 20 feet apart.
- Person #1 takes 3 running steps and overhand passes to the person in the opposite group (#2). Immediately after passing, #1 must sprint backward to get to the end of the line.
- #2 should run toward the ball, take 3 steps, pass and then sprint backward.
- This should go on for a set amount of time.
- Make sure you have cones to establish starting point or the groups will get too close.

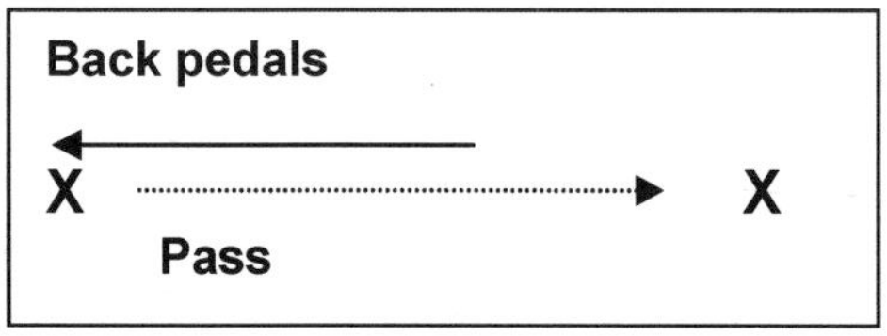

Pass Tag
Equipment: Ball per pair
Group Size: Pairs
Description:

- Have partners face each other.
- When the music starts, the partners begin performing any of the passes used in team handball.
- When the music stops, the person with the ball attempts to tag the partner with the ball (may not throw the ball).
- Walking only is allowed.

Bubba's Keeper
Equipment: 1 Ball and 4 cones per group
Group Size: Pairs
Description:

- Set up cones to mark off 2 goal areas about 15 feet apart.
- Keeper A tries to throw the ball into B's goal area and visa versa.
- The first keeper to score wins.
- Rotate to a new field.

Variation

- Give both keepers a ball.

Defensive Movement
Work on the following drills to improve defensive positioning.

Partner shuffles – Partners face each other standing in a ready position with knees bent. Put hands up slightly in front of their shoulders. Place hands flat against the partner's hands. Without losing contact, shuffle sideways the width of the court for 30 seconds. Change direction for another 30 seconds.

Three passes and check - Partners face each other about 10 to 15 feet apart. The partners make three passes. On the third pass, whoever does not have the ball quickly steps up and plays defense before partner can shoot. Groups just shoot into the wall.

Step out and check drill – In groups of 3, two people stand facing the other person. When one of the two players slaps the ball, the single person should slide over and get directly in front of the person with the ball. When the person raises the ball to shoot, the single person should step up and check the player. When the person with the ball is checked, s/he should pass it to the other person. The single person immediately recovers and diagonally slides to the other person. This process continues for 30 second then individuals rotate positions.

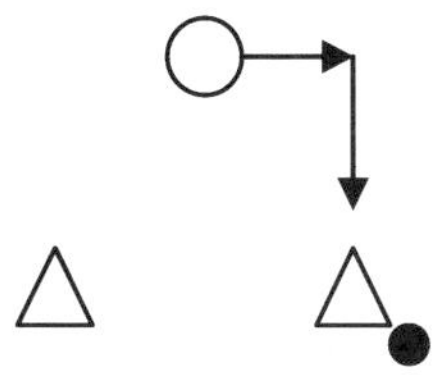

Shooting option

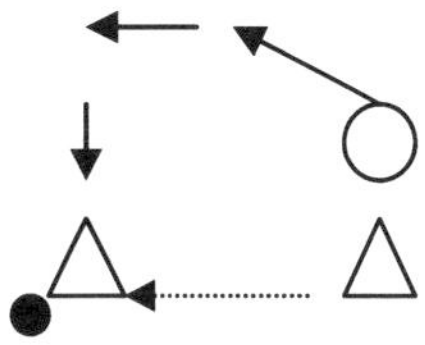

Checked option

Game

End Line Handball

Equipment: Nerf ball per game, pinnies, and endline markers
Group Size: Teams of 4 or 5
Description:

- The game is similar to keep away.
- Teams move the ball up and down the court with passes only. No dribbling, but individuals may take 3 steps at any time.
- If the ball is dribbled, then it is immediately turned over to the other team.
- A team scores one point when the ball is caught behind the end line. The ball may not be run over with the 3 steps.
- After each goal, the defense takes the ball in bounds behind the end line.

Hoop Ball

Equipment: Ball per group, 2 hoops per group, pinnies
Group Size: Groups of 4
Description:

- The object of the game is to have one of the team's players catch the ball while standing in the hoop. Both feet must be inside the hoop.
- The ball is advanced down the court by passing only – no dribbling. Students can take 3 steps and hold the ball for only 3 seconds.
- No defense may be played in the goal area and offense is not allowed to stand in the goal area for more than 3 seconds.

Two Team Keep Away

Equipment: 2 Balls per field, pinnies
Group size: 6
Description:

- Use 2 small grid fields per group.
- One grid should contain the following configuration – 4 red players and 2 blue players and the other grid should have 2 red players and 4 blue players.
- The four players are the offensive players and try to make 5 consecutive passes. If this happens, the offensive team earns 1 point.
- The 2 defensive players try to steal the ball and make two consecutive passes. If this option happens, the defensive team earns 1 point.
- Play 2-minute games and rotate people on the fields.

Pinball

Equipment: Empty tennis cans and 1 ball per group
Group size: 4 to 5
Description:

- Place the 4 tennis cans (pins) along the goal line of each team.
- No one is allowed in the goal area (offense of defense), except to reset the pin.
- The object is to knock down the pins to score a point.
- Play 3-minute games and rotate teams.

6 Goal Handball

Equipment: Ball for every group (color-code the ball), goal area, 5 colored flags for each group, pinnies.
Group Size: 4 to 5
Description:

- Assign each team a different color (red, blue, green, black, yellow, white).
- The object is for the teams to score a goal in every other team's goal.
- If there are 4 on a group, 1 person is the goalie and the other 3 are on offense. If there are five, then 1 person can remain with the goalie to play defense.
- Once a team scores, they take one of the color flags from a cone located behind the goal area of the team upon which they just scored.
- Once a team has collected all 5 colors, reset the flags and change positions of the players. Restart a new game.

Castleball

Equipment: 2 cones and 3 balls per group
Group size: 4 to 5 per team
Description:

- Place a ball on top of each cone (castle). Put one castle in each goal area.
- No one is allowed in the goal area (offense or defense), except to reset the castle.
- The object is to knock the ball off the cone to score a point.
- Play 3-minute games and rotate teams.

Trio Ball
Equipment: 1 Ball per area, goal area marked off
Group Size: 5
Description:

- The object is for 3 offensive players to attempt to score on 2 defensive players (1 defensive player and 1 goalie).
- Use small areas with goals marked on walls or through the use of cones.
- Have each group of 5 select the position they would like to play for the first round. The 3 offensive players from each group will rotate to the game to the right and play against that team's defense.
- Play games for 2 minutes and rotate the offensive players to new team.
- Keep a cumulative score.
- When offensive players return to their home court, the players exchange positions and go another series of games.

5 on 5 Team Handball Game
Equipment: 1 Ball per game, pinnies, and goal markers
Group size: 5
Description:

- Regulation team handball rules with 5 per team. The goalie is included in the five.

Rules

1. The playing rules are in 3's: 3 steps with the ball, 3 seconds holding the ball, 3 dribbles. The ball must be patted down, not carried like a basketball. The sequence of events with the ball can be catch, 3 steps, dribble, catch, 3 steps.
2. A goal is scored when the ball passes completely over the back line within the goal.
3. The goalkeeper is the only player allowed to play the ball in the goal area. The goalie is the only player allowed to contact the ball with his/her feet (but only to save a goal).
4. You may not use arms to block, but may use the torso. Team handball is basically a no arms game.

Unique Sports

Unique Sports

Unique Team Sports

The team sports listed in this section are considered unique for several reasons.

- The activities may combine rules and skills from two or more sports.
- The activities may use new equipment.
- The activities may present activities that are common in other cultures, but not in the American culture.

When these activities are presented, the focus of the teacher should include the following:

1. Working together as a team. Provide the students with opportunities for leadership and followership.
2. Developing a strategy - Have the group devise a strategy they think is effective. The group should be able to transfer their knowledge from the other team sports and develop one that is appropriate for the new team sport.
3. Enhancing health-related fitness. Make sure to check the heart rate at various times during the activities.
4. Using only positive comments and words of support. Students should be told the feedback they provide to their teammates and to the other team must be positive and supportive. While this process may seem artificial, explain to the students that performance is improved when positive, rather than negative comments are provided.

Quad Ball

Equipment: 1 or 2 Nerf balls, 12 empty tennis cans, pinnies

Group Size: 5 to 8

Description:

- Set six tennis cans on each of the base lines.
- The objective is to score as many points as possible.
- Scoring can occur in four ways:
  1. Throwing a touchdown pass (ball is caught on a fly behind the end line). A touchdown from a pass thrown in Area #1= 1 point, Area #2 = 2 points, Area #3 = 3 points.
  2. Knocking down the tennis cans = 1 point per can.
  3. Shooting the ball at a basket from inside the lane = 2 points.
  4. Shooting the ball at a basket from outside the lane = 3 points.
- No dribbling or running with the ball is allowed. Players are not allowed to take more than 3 steps with the ball at any time.
- Players may only hold the ball 5 seconds after they receive a pass.
- If the ball is dropped, the ball must be played like a soccer ball until someone converts it to an aerial ball (lift from foot directly to a hand catch).
- If the ball touches the floor and player picks it up, a free kick is given to the other team at the spot of the violation.
- No fouls (usual fouls in basketball) are allowed. If a foul occurs, a free kick is awarded to the other team at the spot of the foul.

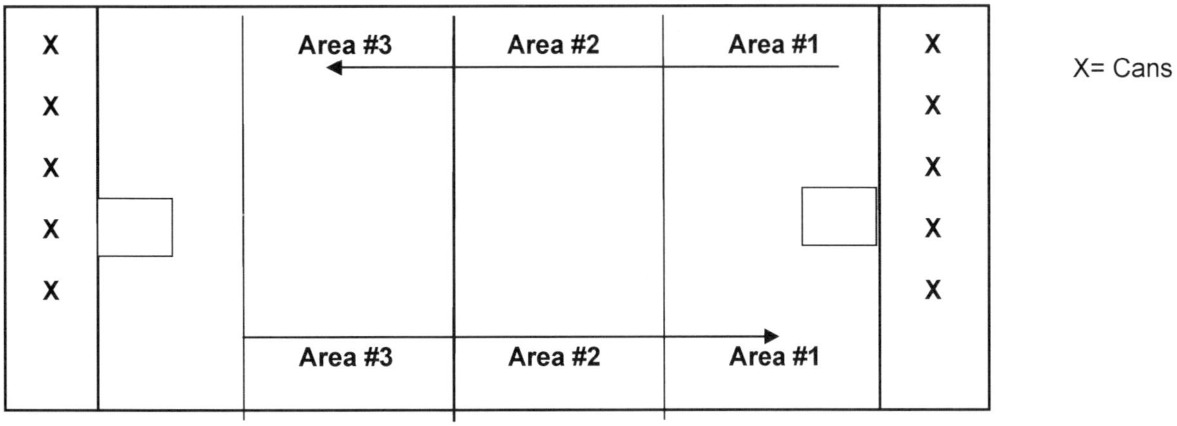

Double Frisbee

Equipment: 2 Frisbees per badminton court
Group size: 4
Description:

- Use the badminton courts and nets as boundaries.
- At the beginning of each point, each team should have one Frisbee.
- The back right person from each team has a Frisbee and simultaneously tosses the Frisbee across the net.
- The object is to toss the Frisbees back and forth as quickly as possible. If one Frisbee is dropped or goes out of play, leave it until both Frisbees are out of play.
- Score one point for each Frisbee the opposite team let drop on their side. The Frisbee must fall inside court boundaries to count as a point.
- Rotate positions with each point.

Frisbee Hoop Ball

Equipment: Hula hoops, Frisbees, pinnies
Group size: 5 to 8
Description:

- Hang a hula-hoop from the basketball basket. Use as many courts as the gym will allow.
- Have two teams challenge each other at a basket.
- The object is to score a goal by tossing the Frisbee through the hula-hoop. The Frisbee cannot be dunked or placed through the hoop. The Frisbee must be thrown through the hoop.
- The game starts with one team in possession of the Frisbee. They toss and catch to the other teammates. If the Frisbee is dropped, the team that gets to it the quickest has possession.
- The team without the Frisbee is defending the goal and trying to intercept passes.
- If two people on opposite teams grab the Frisbee at the same time, they yell "Toss." Both individuals must release the Frisbee into the air.
- Once a goal is scored, the other team gets the Frisbee and immediately attempts to score.
- Play the game in 3-minute quarters.

Ultimate Frisbee

Equipment: 1 Frisbee per game, pinnies, goal line markers

Group size: 5 to 8

Description:

- The object is to score a goal by tossing the Frisbee across an end line or goal line and having a teammate catch it without dropping it.
- The game starts with one team in possession of the Frisbee. They toss and catch to other teammates. If the Frisbee is dropped, the team that gets to it the quickest has possession.
- The team without the Frisbee is defending the goal and trying to intercept passes.
- If two people on opposite teams grab the Frisbee at the same time, they yell, "Toss." Both individuals must release the Frisbee into the air.
- Once a goal is scored, the other team gets the Frisbee and immediately tries to score on the other goal.
- Play the game in 3-minute quarters.

Omni Ball
Equipment: Omnikin Ball, pinnies
Group size: 4
Description:

- Have the teams decide a team color. Each team must have a different color.
- The object of the game is to score a point by having the ball hit the ground.
- The players may not block or interfere in anyway with the other teams that are trying to get to the ball.
- All team members of the color serving must be touching (not holding) the Omnikin ball. The server shouts "omnikin" and calls a color. The team that has their color called must run and receive the ball without dropping it or letting it hit the floor.
- This team now serves the ball as quickly as possible and calls another color.
- A player who catches the ball can pass to a teammate or get everyone on the team together to serve.
- If the team whose color was called drops the ball, the serving team gets a point and gets to serve again.
- The game continues without any stops after points and serves.

Doubles Z Ball

Equipment: Z-ball per group of 4

Group size: Pairs

Description:

- Mark off the court as illustrated below.
- One pair puts the ball into play to another pair by underhand tossing the ball into the square.
- If the serving team misses the square, the other team gets to serve.
- The receiving team must catch the ball as soon as possible. The number of times the ball bounces before the receiving team catches the ball is the number of points the serving team is awarded. For example, if the receiving team requires 5 bounces before catching the ball, then the serving team gets 5 points.
- The server must stand behind the serving line when serving.
- Teams alternate serves after each play.
- Play to 21.

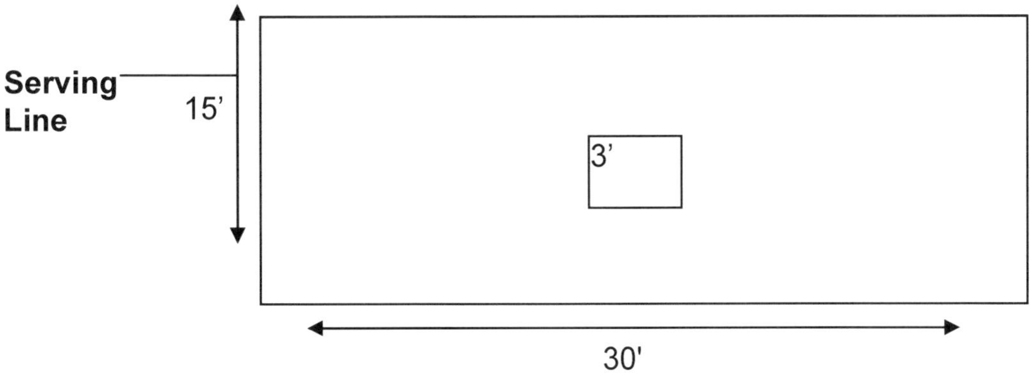

Modified Speed Cricket

Equipment: Flat bats (2 per game), 1 ball per game, and 2 cones per game

Group Size: 6 per group

Description:

- Set up the field as illustrated below.
- Rules
    1. Six outs per inning.
    2. Change batting pairs after every out.
    3. Bat in pairs.
    4. Each batter gets one pitch from the bowler (pitch must be hittable).
    5. Fielding team can put the batting pair out by:
        - Touching the ball with the wicket before the runner gets to the wicket.
        - Catching the ball on a fly
        - The batter missing the pitch.
        - The batter hitting the wicket with the bat when swinging.
- The pitch may be hit on the fly or on 1 bounce.
- Batters must run on every hit ball.
- Batting pairs must switch bases and cannot remain at his/her starting base.
- No foul balls.

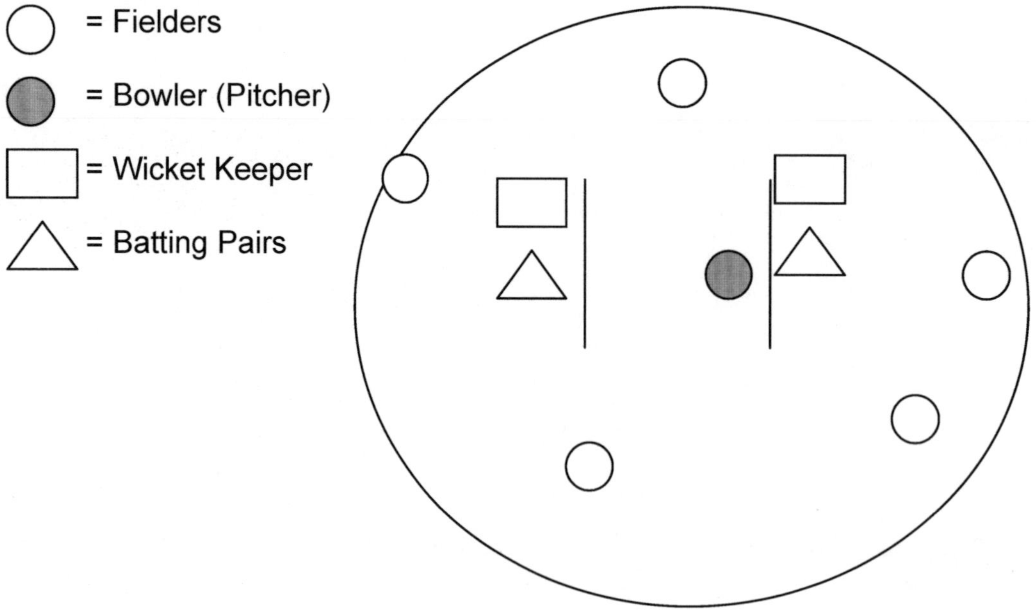

One Goal Soccer

Equipment: Nerf soccer balls, pinnies, goal marks

Group size: 8

Description:

- The game combines soccer and team handball. It is played on a basketball court with a soccer ball.
- There are 8 or more players on a team. The team is divided into half. Half of the team becomes court #1 players. The other half of the team becomes court #2 players.
- All players are on the court all the time, but are restricted to either court #1 or court #2. No players may cross the half court line.
- Court #1 is played like team handball with the players allowed to move the ball by dribbling or passing. Recovery steps are allowed.
- Court #1 players' objective is to maneuver the ball so that their team is the last team to have touched the ball to the wall.
- Court #1 players must get the ball across half court to their court #2 players. Only court #2 players can score.
- Court #2 is played like soccer. NO players are allowed in the goalie area except the two goalies.
- The court #2 players' objective is to score by kicking the ball in the goal.
- Scoring: A team may score only if they were the last team to have touched the ball to the wall on court #1. A team may score only by a court #2 player kicking a goal.

Comments:

1. Switch ends after each score. This allows a student to play both the soccer and team handball ends of the game.
2. Players have to pay close attention so they know whether they are offense or defense.
3. The goalies have to be ready to move into the goalie area and play defense or to move out of the area and play offense.
4. After a goal, the ball is put in play at half court by the team that did not score with both teams having to take the ball to the wall on court #1 before either team can score.
5. One person cannot totally dominate the whole game as is possible in soccer or team handball.

Broomball

Equipment: Broomballs or small 5" balls, short brooms, pinnies and goals
Group Size: 6 per team
Description:

- The object is to **push not strike** the ball into the goal. Teams must shoot from outside the circle.
- To make brooms, use short brooms and duck tape the bristles together.
- The game is played like ice hockey.
- Although best played on ice or snow, this game can be played on sand, grass, asphalt or the gym floor.

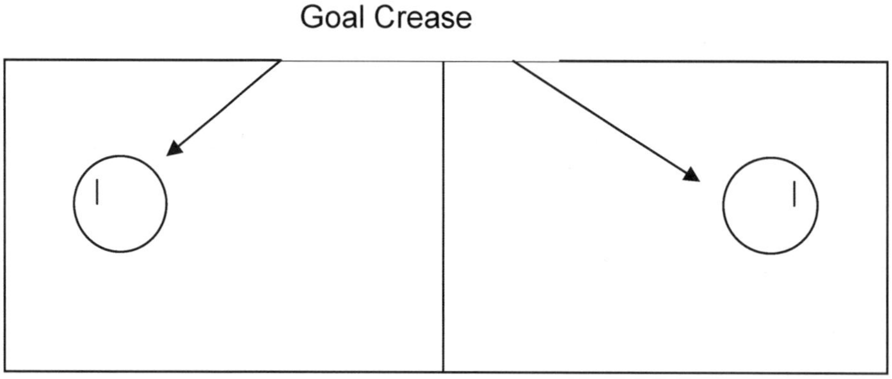

Touch Rugby

Equipment: 1 Football per game, pinnies
Group size: 7
Description:

- The object of the game is to score a touchdown by placing the ball on the ground in the end zone.
- Commencement of Play
    1. Play begins with one player from the offensive team performing a tap back at the center of the field. The defending team must be behind the 10-meter line.
    2. Tap back is used after a touchdown. A tap back is done at midfield. The center puts his/her foot on the ball and pushes it backward to the acting half.
- General play
    1. The ball may be passed or handed to any teammate who is positioned behind the ball carrier (onsides) but it may not be passed or handed in a forward direction.
    2. The ball carrier may run until contact is made with an opponent or a touchdown is scored.
    3. A rollback is performed after every touch. To perform a rollback, place the ball on the ground and roll it back between the legs with one hand to the acting half. All players on the defending team must be 5 meters away.
    4. The acting half may run with the ball, but if s/he is touched, the possession is lost, whether it is the first touch or the sixth touch.
    5. If the ball is dropped and hits the ground at any time during play, the possession is changed and a rollback is executed to start play.
- Offside rules
    1. The defending team must be positioned at least 10 meters down field from the tap back (start of the game).
    2. All defending players must stand 5 meters back from the rollback and cannot move forward until the acting half touches the ball.
    3. Offensive attacking players are considered offside if they are standing in front of the passer and may not legally receive a pass (loss of 1 down).
- Performing a touch
    1. The offensive team has up to 6 downs to score. If, after the sixth down, the offense has not scored, the defensive team takes possession of the ball where the last touch occurred.
    2. All touches must be made with a minimum of force and may be with one or two hands on any part of the body.
    3. The player touched must bring the ball back into play with a rollback at the place where the touch occurred.
    4. A player cannot pass the ball after a touch has occurred.
- Scoring
    1. A touchdown is awarded when a player places the ball on the ground on or over the attacking team's score line without being touched.
    2. An acting half cannot score off a rollback. At least one pass must be made before a touchdown can occur.

Saceasi - (Sac-uh-see)

This equipment is the "non-foot" person's hackey sack. It is a flat, round hackey sack type of material. It is played with the back of the hand or any other part of the body. It may never be held or caught like a ball.

Basic Play

- With a group of two or more, toss and catch the Saceasi to and from other players. Players are only allowed to use the back of their hands. When caught, the player must immediately release it to another player. Play for points.
- Points are awarded when a person drops the Saceasi, or when s/he makes a bad toss. A bad toss is determined by a consensus of the other players. Players do not want to get points. The number of points in a game is determined by the members of the group that are playing
- Another way to play is by creating boundaries (circular or square) and only allowing the players to play within those bounds. Therefore, if any player tries to catch the Saceasi and steps out of bounds, then that player gets a point. Keep in mind, an opposing player can throw the Saceasi out of bounds, but it must be within a reasonable length or in catching distance of the other player.

Definition of a Catch

- As a student watches the Saceasi fall, s/he must position his/her hand to move at the speed of the falling Saceasi, thus lessening the contact force.
- Unlike certain foot games where the foot moves towards the object to project it upward; Saceasi involves moving with the falling object to receive it and then immediately releasing it. A Saceasi is not struck, but briefly caught and released (by a multitude of tosses). The back of the hand should form a spatula-like-platform that Saceasi land on.

Definition of a Release

- The Saceasi, may not be held. Catching and receiving becomes one fluid and continuous motion.

Most Common Mistakes

- **Trying to bat the object**
    1. Unlike most games where the participants try to make contact with the object in play to try to project it forward, the Saceasi requires its players to watch the way the Saceasi falls and gently receive it on the back of the hand. Immediately release the Saceasi using any number of the unique moves or tosses.

- **Not watching how it falls**
  1. Most players believe that if they stick their hand out the Säceasi should adhere to their hand. Just like catching a football, one must reduce the contact force between the hands and the ball by moving the hands in the direction the ball is traveling. The same holds true for the Säceasi. Move the hand in the direction the Säceasi is falling in order to reduce any bounce from the Säceasi. In other words, give with the catch.

Cool Moves with the Saceasi

- **Starfish**
  1. The fingers spread to achieve a wider landing zone. Catch the Saceasi up on knuckles of the hand, not with the back of fingers
- **Whooping Crane (WC)**
  1. The WC toss appears to be a straight toss, but at the last minute, a sideways thrust of the hand, surprises the challengers. Basically, it looks like the person is going to throw straight ahead, but then throws off to the side.
- **Twister**
  1. Spin and turn never allowing time for the opponents to reposition their stance. Fake left and spin right, or vice versa. This shifting of position will surely fool opponents.

Lead-up Games

Sumo Saceasi

Equipment: 1 Saceasi and 1 hula-hoop per pair

Group Size: Pairs

Description

- Both people start with one foot in the hoop. One foot must remain in the hoop when catching.
- The object is to make a catchable throw and have the other person step out side of the hoop as s/he catches.
- If the person does step outside or drops the bag, then that person gets an S. The first one to spell Sumo loses.

4 Square Saceasi
Equipment: Basic four square layout and Saceasi per group
Group Size: 4 to 6
Description:

- Played just like four square but with Saceasi skills.
- The person in the 1 square serves and then any one can toss to any other square.
- The person that misses goes to the 4 square.

Highest Toss and Catch
Equipment: Saceasi per pair
Group size: 2
Description:

- This is a simple activity to see which pair can toss the Saceasi the highest and catch it.
- Catches may be made with two hands.

Volleyball

Volleyball

Volleyball

Skill Progression

1. Forearm pass
2. Overhead set
3. Spike
4. Serve - underhand, sidearm, overhand
5. Blocks
6. Dinks

Ball Handling Activities

Basic Ball Handling Series

- Throws and catches in window while on back
- Throws and catches in window to partner from a standing position
- Throws and catches in window - 1/2 and full turns
- Throws and catches in window to partner from a kneeling position
- Sets to partner
- Set shuffle
- Sets to partner - touch knees, touch shoes, touch floor
- Set ball to self over net (set, duck under, set, duck under)
- Bump to self
- Bump to wall
- Bump to partner
- Bump and set to partner
- Bump shuffle sideways
- Bump shuffle forward and back

Setter Challenge Series

Equipment: 1 ball per pair
Group size: Pairs
Description:

- The pair attempts to complete the following series while setting to each other.
  1. Touch waist
  2. Touch knees
  3. Touch ankles
  4. Touch floor with hands
  5. Kneel on one knee and then stand
  6. Kneel on two knees and then stand
  7. Sit down and stand up
  8. Lie down and stand up

Jump Rope and Set

Equipment: Jump ropes for every student and volleyball for each pair
Group Size: Pairs
Description:

- Have each student get a jump rope and volleyball.
- On signal, the students begin to jump rope for 1 minute.
- After one minute, the pairs pick up volleyball and set back and forth for one minute.
- Continue this process for a total of 10 minutes.

Partner Setting Tasks

Equipment: 1 Ball per pair
Group size: Pairs
Description:

- Give each pair a task sheet or post them around the gym. They need to complete as many as they can in 5 minutes.
  1. Partner pass: Player with the ball, tosses the ball to self; then sets to the partner. The partner catches the ball above the head and sets back.
  2. Target Passing: One partner sets the ball to the target ten times. The partner retrieves the ball. Change roles and repeat.
  3. Basket Volley: One partner stands at the free-throw line on the basketball court. S/he attempts to set the ball into the basket. Take ten sets and change roles.
  4. Sit 'n volley: Partners should be about 12' feet apart, sitting facing each other. The set the ball back and forth to each other. Continue until the pair can get 15 consecutive sets.
  5. Reaction Volley: One person stands with his/her back to the partner. Other person is about 12' away with the ball. The person with the ball sets to the partner and yells "Go." The person must turn around quickly to set the ball back to partner. Repeat 10 times and reverse roles.
  6. Pass and Go, One Line: One person stands with his/her back to a line on the floor, facing partner. The person with the ball sets the ball to the partner, turns and runs and touches the line and runs back to volley the ball back. Continue for 1 minute. Switch roles.
  7. Pass and Go, Two Lines: Same as above, except both people turn to run and touch the line after each set.
  8. Three-line volley: Groups of three form a line about 3 feet apart. Player A volleys to B. Player B volleys back to A, who volleys a long pass over to player C; C volleys a short pass to B, who volleys back to C.

Juggling
Equipment: Ball for every person or every two people
Group size: Individual
Description:

- For 30-seconds, have the students juggle (6" taps above the head).
- Works on ball control and arm strength.

High Low
Equipment: Ball for every person or every two people
Group size: Individual
Description:
- The students should hit a 6" tap and then a 10 ' volley.
- The students should continue for 30 seconds, rest and repeat.

Skill Drills

Sets to Partner
Equipment: Ball for every two people
Group size: Pairs
Description:
- Partners should stand on opposite sides of net. Net height should be about 6' .
- Partners set back and forth. As they set, they must keep their hands above their head.

Partner Shuffle
Equipment: Ball for every pair
Group Size: Pairs
Description:
- Person #1 tosses the ball to the right or left side of the partner.
- The partner slides over and the bumps ball back to the partner.
- Continue for 30 seconds and switch.
- Have partners gradually increase the distance of the slide.

Volley
Equipment: 1 Ball per pair
Group Size: Pairs
Description:
- Pairs find a wall space. If there is not ample wall space, have the students play against another pair.
- The first partner bumps the ball to the wall. S/he runs in back of his/her partner. The second partner then bumps and runs in back of the partner.
- This process continues until one of the pair misses. The person who misses gets a "V".
- Play until one partner spells VOLLEY.

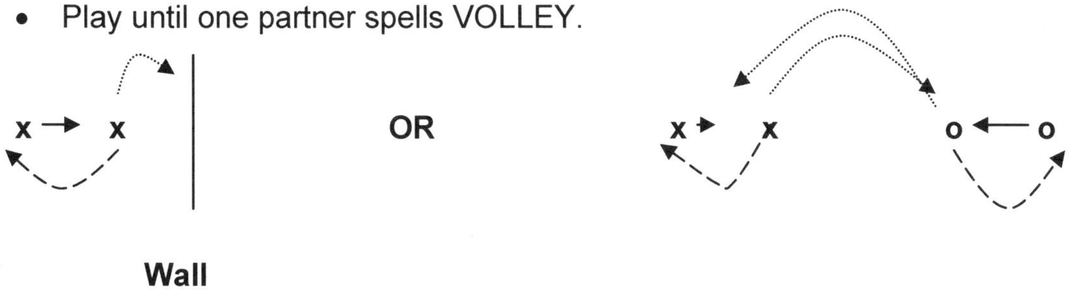

Circle Volleyball
Equipment: 1 Volleyball per group
Group size: 5
Description:

- Have one team challenge another team.
- One of the teams forms a circle and is the offensive team.
- The other team is the defensive team and forms a circle on the inside of the offensive team.
- The offensive team puts one of their team members in the middle of the defensive circle.
- The game is started with an offensive player who sets the ball to another teammate. It may not be passed to the center person on the first hit.
- The object of the game is to set the ball to the center person and have that person set it back without the defensive team getting the ball.
- Change the middle persons every 30 seconds and change offensive and defensive team every 2 minutes.

● Offensive Team

○ Defensive Team

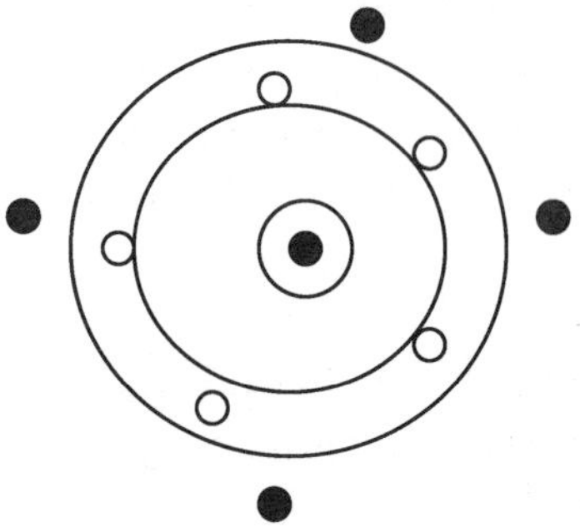

Volleyball on the Move
Equipment: Jump ropes and volleyballs
Group size: 4
Description:

- Have 2 students hold the ends of the jump rope at about waist level. This makes a low net.
- The other two group members are setting or bumping the ball over the makeshift net.
- As the students' skills improve, the people holding the net can begin to slowly move. This forces the hitters to adjust and to move.
- Go for one minute and switch places.

Volleyball Golf

Equipment: 1 Ball per pair, poly spots or cones scattered around the gym to mark tee off spot

Group size: Pairs

Description:

- The object of this activity is to practice accuracy in setting by setting the ball into basketball goals.
- Have the pairs begin on any of the poly spots or cones in the gym.
- One person sets ball. If it goes in, the partner sets from cone. If it is missed, the person runs to retrieve ball and set from where the ball is recovered.
- Count the number of sets it takes to get the ball in the basket.
- Compete against a partner and then challenge another person.

Tip and Run

Equipment: 1 Ball per game

Group Size: 4 to 6

Description:

- Have both teams start at the spiking line on opposite sides of the net.
- All volleys must be played between these two lines.
- The ball is tossed over the net to begin and then rallied.
- Once a person tips the ball, s/he must run and touch the back line of the court before returning to the game.
- Play 5-point games and rotate teams.

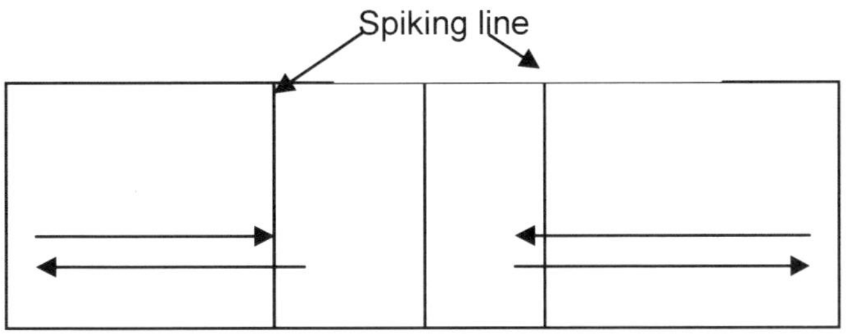

Ball Bump Challenge
Equipment: Volleyballs
Group Size: Groups of 5 to 7
Description:

- One person is the leader in front of group with the volleyball. The leader bumps the ball to anyone in the group.
- The object is to knock the leader out by having everyone in the group bump ball. No one may hit it again until everyone in the group has touched it.
- If the ball hits the ground or if anyone hits it twice in a row, then the leader gets a point and stays in front.

Set and Run
Equipment: 1 Ball per group
Group size: 4
Description:

- Have one team stand opposite another team on small courts. Badminton courts work well.
- One person sets ball to the opposite team and then runs to touch the back line before s/he can set the ball again.
- Play rounds of 5 points or for 2 minutes.
- Rotate and play a new team.

Yo Yo Drill
Equipment: 1 Ball per pair
Group Size: Pairs
Description:

- Put one partner up at the net (backs to the net) with the ball. The other person starts at the baseline.
- On a signal, the person with the ball tosses the ball up in a big arch.
- The person on the baseline runs forward to bump the ball back to the passer and then runs backward to the baseline and begins again.
- Go for 30 seconds and switch places.
- On the next round, the tosser stands at the net and the passer at the 10 foot line.
- The tosser tosses a ball over the head of passer. The passer slides back and bumps the ball back to tosser.
- Go for 30 seconds and switch places.

Volleyball Pick-up

Equipment: One volleyball and ten bean bags for each group

Group size: 5 to 7

Description:

- Each group should form a large circle. Place ten beanbags in the center of the circle.
- The object of the activity is for each group to remove all of the beanbags from the center of the circle.
- In order to complete this task, the group members begin to volley the ball back and forth.
- After the fifth consecutive hit, the group can begin to remove the bean bags from the circle.
- Anyone in the group can run to the center and take one beanbag.
- Once that person brings a beanbag back to the outside of the circle, another person may enter the circle for another beanbag.
- The group must keep setting or bumping the ball while the beanbags are being removed.
- If the ball hits the ground, the group must return the beanbags to the center.

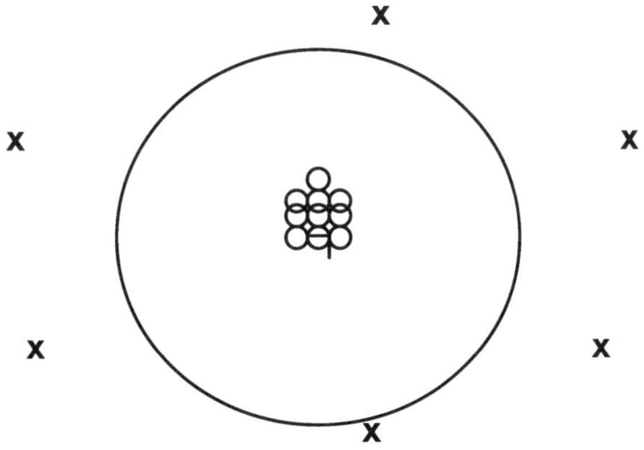

Boo Boo Drill

Equipment: 1 Ball per group

Group Size: 3

Description:

- Start with a challenger's side and a champ's side. Have a group of 3 on each side of the net with a group of 3 waiting behind the challenger's side.
- The group on the champs' side is lying down on backs or on their knees (depending on skill level).
- One player on the waiting team throws the ball down on the ground so that it bounces high on the champ's side.
- The players on the champ's side get up quickly to play the ball and then play 3 on 3 until someone misses.
- If the challengers win, they run to the other side and get on their knees or back and the waiting team runs into challenger's side.
- If the champs win, the challengers exit and the waiting team comes into the challenger's side.

Setter Triangle
Equipment: 1 Ball per group
Group size: 4
Description:

- 3 people arrange themselves in a triangle.
- A fourth person stands behind the person with the ball.
- The person with the ball sets the ball and then follows the set (covering).
- The person receiving the ball must touch the floor and then set to the next person and follow the set.

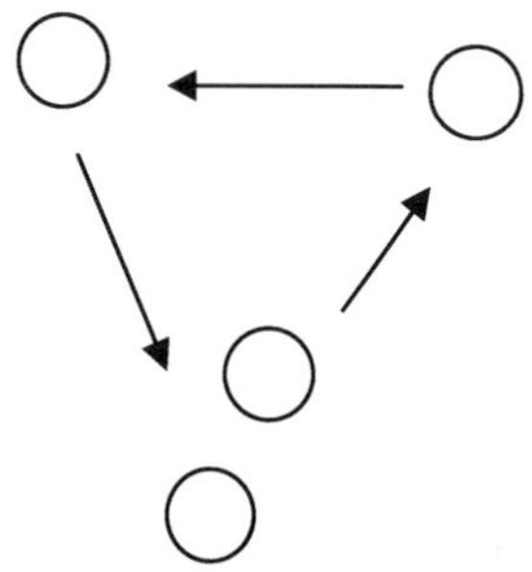

Dead Fish Serving
Equipment: Volleyballs for every other person
Group size: 6
Description:

- This is a serving drill. The object is not to leave any "dead fish" on the court.
- Both teams serve continuously.
- If a person misses the serve, s/he must go to the opposite side and sit in one of the court positions.
- These "dead fish" cannot serve again until one of their teammates sends a ball over to him or her and that person catches it.
- The team with the least "dead fish" after a determined amount of time is declared the winner.

Limbo Serving
Equipment: 1 ball per group
Group Size: 3
Description:

- Each team should put the ball on the 10' spiking line to begin and challenge another group of 3 stands opposite them across the net.
- The first person in each line runs and picks up the ball, runs back to the service line and serves the ball. After the person serves, s/he goes to the back of the line and helps retrieve balls from teammates
- The second person in line takes off as soon as the first person picks up the ball from the 10' line.
- This continues until one team scores 10 good serves.

3's Serving
Equipment: 1 Ball per group
Group Size: 3
Description:

- Each team should have 2 people on one side of the net and 1 person on the other.
- The side with 2 people has the ball and begins the action.
- The first person underhand serves the ball to the other side and then runs under the net to the other side.
- The person on the other side retrieves the ball, gets behind the service line and serves the ball back and runs under the net.
- This process continues for 1 minute.
- See how many serves each group can get in that period. Only count the ones that go over.
- Have groups attempt to beat their own score the next time.
- If students cannot serve from the base line, move them closer.

Hopscotch Volley:
Equipment: Hopscotch board on the wall, 1 ball per group
Group size: 2 or 4 depending upon the number of hopscotch boards
Description:

- Tape the Hopscotch board on the wall. Hopscotch squares are 3' x 3' squares. Buy poster board or dots on the wall work well.
- Have partners take turns attempting to hit the squares in order, moving from number one to eight and back.
- Challenge a different person after the game is complete.

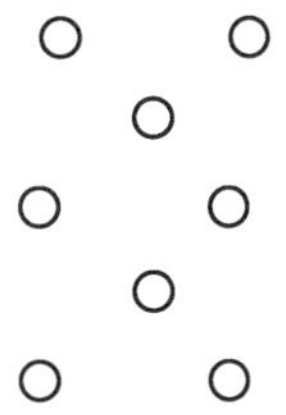

Volleyball Pepper
Equipment: 2 Balls per group
Group Size: 3
Description:

- Have two players (tossers) stand about 10' apart and about 6' away from the receiver.
- The receiver slides between the two tossers, taking tosses and returning good passes back to the tossers for 1 minute.
- To encourage good passes, set a minimum number to be acquired.
- After 1 minute, switch places.

Volley Flip
Equipment: 1 Ball per group
Group Size: 4 to 8
Description:

- The group should form a semi-circle with 1 person in front of the group.
- Leader sets the ball to anyone in group.
- The object is for everyone in the group to touch the ball and not have the ball touch the ground. The ball must be touched by everyone in the group, may not touch the ground and once a person touches the ball that person may not play it again until the new round.
- If the sequence is completed, then change leaders. If the leader is not complete, then the leader gets one point and sets the ball again.

Block and Shuffle
Equipment: None
Group Size: Pairs
Description:

- Have the partners start on opposite sides of the net at the baseline.
- On signal, the pairs run toward each other and when they get to the net, they jump up and clap hands over the net.
- They should slide along the net and block every 3 steps. When they get to the end of the net, they run backwards and slide along the baseline.
- Repeat for a set amount of time.

Net Block and Run
Equipment: None
Group Size: 4 to 6
Description:

- Have groups of 4 to 6 line up on service line.
- The first person runs forward to net, slides across net doing slides and blocks, runs backward to end line and then slides to end of line.

Spiking Progressions

Equipment: 1 Ball per pair
Group size: Pairs
Description:

- Hit the ball with a spiking motion toward the ground.
- Hit the ball with a spiking motion into the wall.
- Toss the ball and catch it above the head.
- With a partner, have one partner toss the ball. The other person catches it above the head.
- With a partner, have one partner toss ball. The other person spikes it into the wall.

Blocking Progression

Equipment: 1 Ball per pair
Group size: Pairs
Description:

- Blockers stand close to the net. The net should be lowered or use a rope tied about head height for average student.
- The tossers throw ten balls (one at a time) to the blockers.
- The blockers surround the ball with the hands and catch the ball and then toss the ball back to tosser.
- For the next set of ten balls, the blockers surround the balls with their hands and block them down without batting at the ball.
- For the next set of ten balls, the tosser hits the balls at the blocker's hands.

2 on 2 Tip Game

Equipment: 1 Ball per game
Group size: 2
Description:

- Mark off 3 courts per volleyball court.
- Teams play normal volleyball rules but the game is played between the spiking line and the net.
- The reason for calling this activity a tip game is because players will quickly learn that the best way to keep the ball in the small court and score points is to tip the ball.

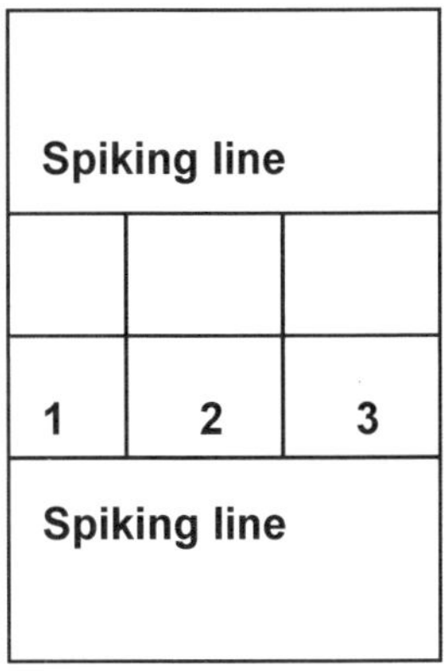

Tip Spot

Equipment: Balls and poly spots
Group Size: 4 or 5
Description:

- Have each group put 4 poly spots down on the ground about 2' to 3' from the net.
- The object is to have one person set the ball to the spiking line. A player tries to tip the ball so that it lands on one of the poly spots.
- Rotate setters and tippers.

Lead-up Games

One Bounce Volleyball
Equipment: 1 Ball per game
Group size: 4
Description:
- The game is played on a badminton court with regulation height net.
- The game is played like regular volleyball with the following exceptions:
  1. The ball can be hit as many times on a side as needed.
  2. The ball can bounce one time on each side.
  3. The ball cannot be spiked. It must be played with a bump only.
  4. The ball is put into play with an underhand serve.
  5. Rally scoring.

Three's
Equipment: 1 Ball per game
Group size: 3
Description:
- Mark off smaller courts. On a regulation volleyball court you could have 3 small courts.
- The game is played between the spiking line and the net.

Rules
  1. The ball is tossed over and then rallied.
  2. The ball can be passed or set. No spiking.
- The game is played for 1 or 2 minutes and then rotate the teams.

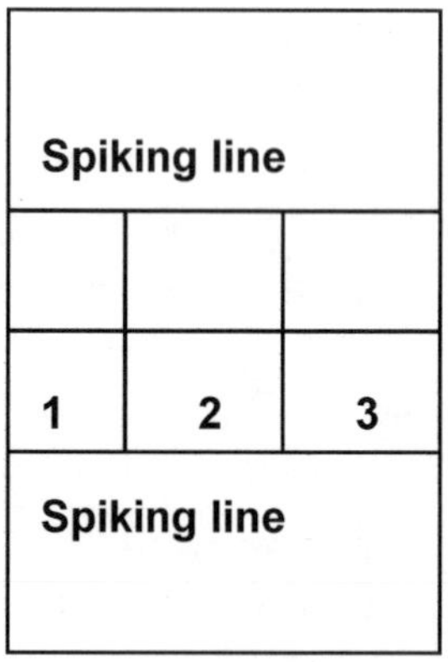

Cross Court Volleyball
Equipment: Volleyballs and badminton nets
Group Size: Groups of 3 to 4 per team
Description:
- Game is played for 3 minutes using volleyball rules on a badminton court. No spiking.
- At the end of three minutes, the teams rotate counterclockwise one court.
- Start a new game immediately.
- Each team keeps the points scored during each game.
- Each team should total up their points at the end of all rounds played during class.

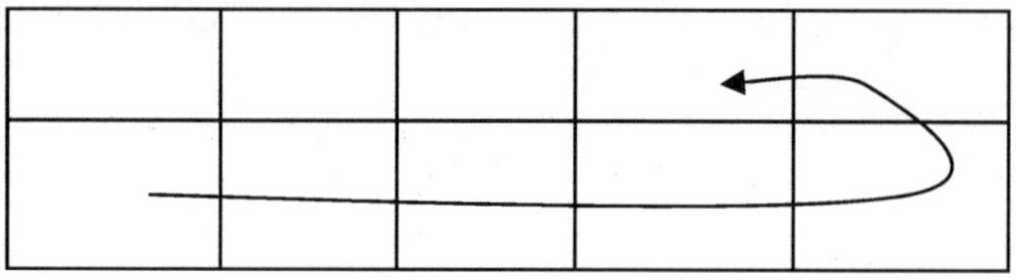

Error Volleyball

- Regular volleyball rules, except when a player makes an error, s/he must leave the court and goes to the error location and completes tasks before returning to the team.
- The team plays short until the player or players return(s).

Prison Volleyball

Equipment: 1 Ball per group
Group Size: 4
Description:

- Use badminton courts.
- The object of this activity is to be the team with the most players at the end of 2 minutes.
- The game starts with one team serving. The teams rally back and forth.
- The player who misses the ball must go to the opposite team.
- The team that lost the player now serves.

Shower Service Ball

Equipment: Numerous volleyballs
Group size: Two equal teams
Description:

- The object of this game is for a team to serve volleyballs over a net without the opposite team catching the serve before it hits the ground.
- Divide the students into two teams (more if court space allows). The teams should be in a scattered formation on opposite sides of the volleyball court.
- To begin the game, one team is given two volleyballs. Anyone from that team can serve. The serve must occur anywhere behind the volleyball end line.
- If the serve clears the net, the opposite team must catch it, run behind their end line and immediately serve it back to the other team. If this team fails to catch it, then the serving team gets a point. If the serve fails to clear the net, the receiving team gets a point.
- After a certain amount of time, start adding volleyballs and continue to add as many volleyballs as safety allows.
- If the students cannot serve from base line, move them closer.

Four Square Volleyball
Equipment: Volleyballs
Group Size: Pairs
Description:

- Make a large four square court or use the badminton service areas.
- Each team occupies a different square area.
- To begin the game, the team in the #1 square serves to any of the other squares.
- The serve must be underhand. After the serve, the teams may use only bumps and sets to keep the ball in play. No spiking is allowed.
- Each team is allowed three hits and then the ball must be sent to another square. If any ball hits the line it is considered in bounds.
- If a pair misses the ball, they leave their square and go to square #4. Everyone else moves up one square.

Variation:

- To increase the challenge level, the rules can be changed so that each team member must hit the ball before sending it to a different square. Spiking is permissible, but not on a serve.

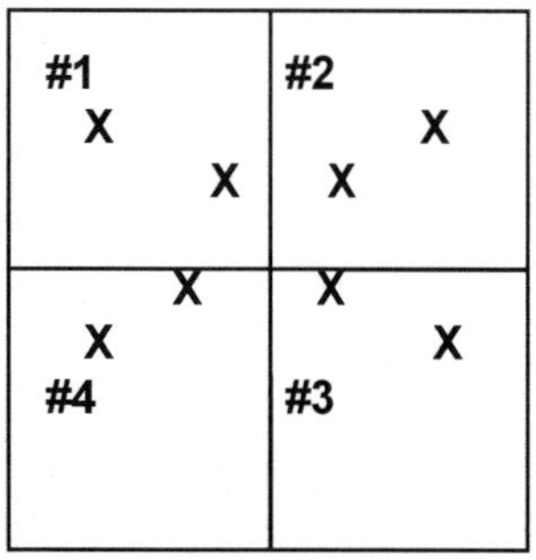

Bucketball
Equipment: 1 Ball per person, container for each group
Group size: Groups of 8
Description:

- The teams of 8 should form a circle around a container.
- On a signal, the teams begin setting the ball to the container.
- The object of the activity is to set the ball into the container. If a ball goes in, leave it and get another ball. If the ball does not go in the container, leave it and a teammate will retrieve.
- The first team to get 6 balls into container yells, "Stop". That team gets one point.
- Play 3 point rounds and then move the students back further from the containers.

Anything Goes Volleyball
Equipment: 1 Ball per game, lowered nets, badminton courts
Group size: 4
Description:

- The game is played on a badminton court with badminton height nets.
- The game is played like regular volleyball with the following exceptions.

Rules

1. The ball can be hit as many times on a side as they want.
2. The ball can bounce one time between hits.
3. The ball cannot be spiked. It must be played with the bump only.
4. The ball is put into play with a toss from backcourt.
5. A team scores any time the other team cannot get the ball over the net.

Go Fishing
Equipment: 1 Ball per group
Group Size: 4
Description:

- One team challenges another team.
- All players, except 1 should have a ball.
- The person without the ball should go on the opposite team's court and sit in the back right area.
- The object of the activity is for the other team members to serve the ball in order for the seated person to catch it.
- Once the ball is caught, the person who served the ball that was caught runs over and takes the seated person's place. This person now sits in the center back area.
- This process continues until the ball is caught in all 6 positions (right back, center back, left back, left front, center front, right front).

3 x 3 x 3 Game
Equipment: 1 Ball per group
Group Size: 3
Description:

- One team is on the challenger's side. The second team of 3 is on the champ's side. The remaining group waits behind the challenger's end line.
- The challengers serve the ball and a rally begins.
- If the challengers win, they run to the other side and the waiting team runs into challengers' side and serves the ball quickly.
- If the champs win, the challengers exit and the waiting team comes into the challenger's side.
- Play for a few minutes and then rotate the teams to other courts.

Skill Point Volleyball

- Played just like regular volleyball, except every time either team puts the ball on the ground with a spike, tip or block they automatically get a point (even if they were not serving).

King/Queen of the Court

Equipment: 1 Ball per court
Group size: 4
Description:

- This is a progressive work-up game in which teams play one minute matches.
- The goal of the game is to work one's way to the king's court and remain in this court by beating challengers.

Rules

- At the beginning of the game, place two teams on each court. Designate one court as the King's Court.
- All winners move toward this court.
- Losers on all courts except the King's Court remain and serve the next point. Winners on the King's Court will remain and serve the next point.
- Losers on the King's Court will go to the end of the line at the beginning of the rotation.
- The rotation to use when playing this game is illustrated below.

King's Court

Court 1	Court 2	Court 3	Court 4	Court 5
King's Court	**Team B**	**Team D**	**Team F**	**Team H**
Net **Team A**	**Team C**	**Team E**	**Team G**	**Team I**

Winners move up to the next court.
Losers stay and serve.
If a team in King's Court loses, they go to the open side on Court #5.

Winners move in this direction

←

4 on 4 Small Court Games

Equipment: 1 Ball per game
Group Size: 4
Description:

- Regular volleyball rules played on badminton courts with regular nets.
- Play rally scoring.